STUDENT GUIDE

AS Media Studies

UNIT 2

AQA

Module 2:
Textual Topics in Contemporary Media

Julia Burton

Philip Allan Updates
Market Place
Deddington
Oxfordshire
OX15 0SE

Tel: 01869 338652
Fax: 01869 337590
e-mail: sales@philipallan.co.uk
www.philipallan.co.uk

ISBN-13: 978-0-86003-929-7
ISBN-10: 0-86003-929-3

This guide has been written specifically to support students preparing for the
AQA AS Media Studies Unit 2 examination. The content has been neither
approved nor endorsed by AQA and remains the sole responsibility of the
authors.

Printed by Raithby, Lawrence & Co. Ltd, Leicester

Environmental information
The paper on which this title is printed is sourced from managed, sustainable
forests.

Contents

Introduction

■ ■ ■

Content Guidance

The Key Concepts

Textual topics

■ ■ ■

Questions and Answers

Introduction

About this guide

This guide is designed to provide information, support and guidance for students following the AQA AS Media Studies course. It specifically focuses on Unit 2, Textual Topics in Contemporary Media, which is examined by a 90-minute examination paper and which counts for 30% of the total AS marks, and 15% of the total A-level marks. There are three sections to this guide:

- **Introduction** — this provides advice on how to use the guide, an outline of the unit and what is being examined, information about how this unit links with the other AS units, an explanation of the skills required for the Textual Topics in the Contemporary Media exam, and advice about how to prepare for the exam.
- **Content Guidance** — the first part of this section provides you with an overview of each of the Key Concepts and shows you how they should be applied to the texts you study within each topic. This conceptual framework is at the heart of all three units in the AS Media Studies course and needs to be understood thoroughly. These concepts are also assessed in the A2 course, so you need to read this information carefully. The second part of the Content Guidance section explains what you need to know and understand about each of the four topic areas for Unit 2, and includes a selection of relevant ideas, debates, theories and information.
- **Questions and Answers** — this provides five sample exam questions, together with answers at grade A and grade C. Examiner's comments are included to demonstrate how marks are awarded and to show you the strengths of each answer and how it could be improved. At the end of each topic, advice is given about how to approach other types of question that might come up on the paper. The section ends with a number of extra questions for you to work through.

How to use the guide

To use this guide properly you need to be systematic. Make sure that you read the Introduction carefully and are fully aware of the exam skills you need for this unit. It is important that you understand how the three AS units interrelate with each other. When you are sure that you have a good understanding of what is required for the exam and are familiar with its format, you should move on to the Content Guidance section.

The Content Guidance section takes you through the requirements for Unit 2, and explains how to explore and examine texts. It deals first with the Key Concepts and gives examples of how to apply each concept to texts. The second part goes into detail about what you should cover for each topic on the paper. There are references to the ideas, theories and information related to each topic that you will need to apply to your case study material. Make notes as you read this section and work on the suggestions given by applying each concept to your own examples, the texts that you have covered in class and other texts of your own that fit within the topic. Fill in any gaps in your knowledge, and make sure that you have applied the Key Concepts to each text you might use in the examination and that you understand relevant topic ideas and information. This process will take some time to complete, but it will ensure that you have covered every aspect of the four topics.

When you have finished your study of the content you should move on to the Question and Answer section, where you will find examples of typical exam questions with grade-A and grade-C answers. Read each question carefully and make a detailed plan of what to include in an answer. Spend about 10 minutes doing this and then write a full answer. Next, study the grade-A answer and the examiner's comments and compare the answer to your own. You could then look at the grade-C answer and decide how it could be improved. Finally, rewrite your own answer to make it grade-A standard.

It is important to notice how the better answers are structured and how well they focus on the question: don't just concentrate on the information they contain. Good answers present an argument supported by textual detail and show understanding of topic ideas. They answer the question set, rather than regurgitating memorised notes, and use the relevant Key Concepts confidently.

You could use some of the essay titles to practise writing timed essays. Your teacher should have a supply of past papers that you can use too. Allow yourself 45 minutes for each essay, and don't forget to plan before you start to write. It makes all the difference to your focus on the question. Five minutes spent planning what to include in your answer is always time well spent.

The AS specification

The aims of the AQA AS Media Studies course are:
- to provide you with a conceptual framework which will give you the critical tools necessary to undertake your own readings of media texts and think about the significance and development of the mass media
- to enable you to engage with theory, research and ideas relating to the media
- to build on, develop and extend your own interests, knowledge and enjoyment of media texts and technologies

You can work out from this list that *your* interests are at the heart of the specification, and that it is designed to encourage **critical autonomy**; in other words, you need to analyse and discuss media texts from your own point of view and not merely learn what others have written about them. The emphasis at AS is on contemporary texts and topics, i.e. what has been produced and talked about in the mass media in the last 5 years.

How Unit 2 links with the other AS units

The three units assessed at AS are: Unit 1, Reading the Media, which accounts for 30% of the total AS marks; Unit 2, Textual Topics in Contemporary Media, which accounts for 30%; and Unit 3, Coursework — Practical Production, which accounts for 20%.

The course consists of a range of concepts, ideas and skills that will help you communicate ideas about the mass media. Unit 2 works alongside Unit 1 and Unit 3 in its conceptual approach to media texts. This is the skill you need for all AS units and counts for 60% of the total mark across the three units. You will be able to apply some of what you have covered in the other AS units to your Unit 2 exam: the textual analysis skills you developed in preparing for Unit 1; and the knowledge and understanding of the topics gained from Unit 3, in researching the Brief, applying textual construction to the product, and deconstruction and evaluation skills.

Unit 2 is also concerned with ideas and theories involved in evaluating texts. Your work on the Practical Production in Unit 3, whether with time-based or page-based technology, should broaden your knowledge of the Unit 2 textual topics and develop your understanding of media technology.

Examinable skills

There are two main skills that the examiner will be assessing in each of your Unit 2 answers. These are:

- being able to apply the Key Concepts (media representations, media languages (including narrative and genre), media audiences, media institutions and media values and ideology to the evaluation of texts
- showing that you can apply and evaluate important ideas, theories, debates and information to texts and topics in contemporary media

Applying the Key Concepts will earn you valuable marks. They are vital to the detailed study of specialised topics in Module 2. You should practise deconstructing your texts, first by considering representation, media languages and audiences and then by thinking about who produced it and what messages about society are conveyed. To show this skill in the examination you will need to have done a thorough analysis beforehand of each text using each concept, so that they are at your fingertips and can be woven into your answer. For more on the Key Concepts, see pp. 13–24.

You will develop the second skill through your study of the media topics. For example:

- **Ideas** — you should have some knowledge of the major ideas which relate to each topic and be able to use them in your answers.
- **Debates** — questions often start with a controversial statement about a topic inviting you to consider a debate around a particular idea.
- **Theories** — you will have looked at some theories and research about narrative and audience, genre and representation for the first three topics in this paper. If you are studying British newspapers, you will have covered theories and ideas

about news values too. You should show the examiner that you have considered these when evaluating your texts.

- **Information** — you will be able to access plenty of information which is relevant to each topic: under the topics British newspapers and advertising and marketing, for example, information about codes of practice, complaints procedure and various facts and figures are available from industry sources and should be built into your study of texts.

A recital of statistics and academic theories will not earn as many marks as the evaluation of texts in the light of the above factors. Ideas, theories, information and debates should cast light on the texts themselves rather than obscure them.

The detailed study of texts within each topic is of paramount importance. In the exam you must show your knowledge and understanding of the texts themselves by giving detailed illustrations. You cannot demonstrate knowledge of media language, for instance, if you write about film or television fiction without giving examples of how the language of the moving image is used.

The skill of writing an essay within a set amount of time is an important requirement for this exam. Your argument should be in direct response to the wording of the question, so spend time analysing the question word by word. Plan each answer carefully, keeping the question in mind. Don't try to rewrite an essay you produced in class or as revision. You will be able to use the case studies and theories etc. that you have revised, but make sure that from your first paragraph you focus on the question asked. Be certain to include comments relevant to the wording of the question at the start of the essay. This doesn't mean that you need a long introduction — get straight to the point(s). In the main body of the essay, you shouldn't repeat any points, so provide textual illustration and/or reference to topic ideas and so on for each point, explain or develop your idea briefly, and then move on to the next line of argument. Remember to use topic terminology wherever you can, but again, avoid unnecessary repetition.

The exam

In the exam you will have to answer two questions in 90 minutes, each taken from a separate topic area. Each question is marked out of 30 so you must allocate your time accordingly. Keep a close eye on the clock.

Use the first 5 minutes of the exam to read through the paper. Choose one question from each of the two topic areas you have prepared. You may have studied more than two topics, in which case you should choose the two questions that fit in best with what you have learned. Each topic area contains two questions which are slightly different in content and focus. For example, if you have studied film and broadcast fiction, one question may ask you to discuss several texts while the other asks for more detail on one text.

Remember to demonstrate the skills that you are being assessed for and choose questions that will allow you to demonstrate them well. All questions are of equal difficulty. If you think one sounds easier than another, read it again to make sure that you have interpreted it correctly. Plan each answer by jotting down case studies, names of theories, terminology and a list of illustrations and examples to include in your answer.

Study skills and revision strategies

After you have covered a topic in class, you will only have the basic material for the examination. You will need to incorporate your own experience of the media and knowledge of media texts in your exam answers. Some advice about the different topics is given below:

- **Film and broadcast fiction**. You may have studied two films and some soap-operas and situation comedies in class. Continue to apply the conceptual framework to the different films and television fiction that you watch. Pay particular attention to moving image techniques, developments in the genre and interesting narrative structure. Make some notes and analyse a scene or two (you may need to record the programme, or rent a DVD or video). By doing this you will be keeping up with contemporary media and practising your skills.

- The same advice applies if you are studying **documentary**. Keep an eye out for old and new documentaries appearing on television or in the cinema and read about them in the listings magazines and online listings. (All terrestrial channels show documentaries and BBC4 and other Freeview or satellite stations are a good source.) Always note the date they were made, the institution responsible and the scheduling. Record them and consider them in the light of documentary and debates. Make notes to store alongside your class texts.

- **Advertising and marketing** is an ongoing activity. After covering the topic in class, keep alert to new campaigns and collect as much textual material from the campaign (print and audio/visual) as you can. Be aware of covert techniques and look out for merchandise and tie-ins when you go shopping or out for a meal. Then research the campaign.

- You need to keep reading **British newspapers**, not just during the term in which you cover the topic. Don't rely on work done in class to revise for the exam. The more up-to-date your case study, the more impressed the examiner will be. Keep yourself informed about changes in ownership, circulation figures, and developments in the content or format of newspapers you have studied.

Consume the media critically, spot what is new and keep an eye on the ways in which media deal with other media. Most broadsheet newspapers have media pages or a media section. Look at the online versions too — there is often more detail there which you can print and keep in your file. Controversial advertising and public relations events and issues regularly make the news on television and radio. Keep notes, with dates, and follow the development of the story.

Frequently asked questions

What do I need to know?

Look at the specification to see what you are expected to have studied. If you cannot find one in your school or college, you can download it from the AQA website (**www.aqa.org.uk**). Past papers and the principal examiner's reports, which discuss strengths and weaknesses of candidates' answers, are also available online.

How long before the exam should I start revising?

You should begin your revision at least 2 months before the start of the exam season. Make sure that you know the date and time of the exam (and all your other exams) and plan a timetable divided into topics. You need plenty of time to study each topic and to revise your analysis of the texts, including the moving image texts.

How will I remember everything?

Short revision sessions work far better than studying for long periods of time. Research shows that the morning is the best time for learning. When you go through your notes, highlight important words and phrases. You can then concentrate on these sections in the week before the exam. Some people find that writing out selected highlights helps them to remember the key information. It is important that your studies remain fresh in your mind.

Revision tips

- During the revision period, discuss the texts with your friends — learn from each other.
- Have plenty of sleep in the week before the exam — at night and not in the day. Get up early when your brain is at its best.
- Keep hydrated (drink plenty of water) and oxygenated (take plenty of fresh air and exercise) to keep mind and body at top performance level.
- Don't allow yourself to panic — keep away from people who are in that mode. Stay calm.

Note: films that have an 18 certificate have been identified with an asterisk. The AQA Media Studies specification allows the use of 18-certified films.

Content Guidance

This section falls into two areas. The first of these is the **Key Concepts** and how to use them to explore texts within each topic. These comprise:

- representations
- media languages and forms (including narrative and genre)
- audiences
- institutions
- values and ideology

You should already have a good knowledge of these Key Concepts and will have practised applying them to print, audio and moving image texts to prepare for the Unit 1 test and for the practical coursework unit.

The second section covers the four **textual topics**, which are:

- film and broadcast fiction
- documentary
- advertising and marketing
- British newspapers

The Key Concepts

'Concepts' is another word for ideas and the Key Concepts for AQA Media Studies form the toolkit necessary to analyse (or take apart) a media text. These critical tools give guidance in what to look for and the questions to ask in order to find out both what the text says and the meanings behind what it says.

In this module, you will be studying two particular media topics and a number of texts that come into these categories. You need to use the following tools to investigate them:
- the language (denotative and connotative levels of meaning)
- who or what is being represented and how this is shown
- the narrative structure and techniques
- how the texts fit in with others in the genre
- the way the texts have been shaped by the institutions that have produced them
- the values which the texts carry
- the audiences to whom they are addressed

The process can be compared to a mechanic looking inside an engine and using different parts of a socket set to take the engine apart. The parts then have to be put back together to assess the way the text works as a whole. While you are making case studies of texts such as films, newspapers or advertising campaigns, you will also be studying various theories, debates and information which will help deepen your understanding of how texts work and will build up a solid knowledge base of the topic itself.

The Key Concepts are assessed in every exam or coursework unit of the AQA AS and A2 Media Studies course. They are the first step on the way to understanding the mass media. You must make sure that you understand what they are and that you learn how to use them. It is important to try to employ them in a way that is natural to you. At first they might seem like a set of rules, but they are not intended to restrict your thinking — instead they are designed to show you how to start thinking about the media. This is a skill that needs to be practised until your reading of texts using the Key Concepts will be natural to you and this will come across to the examiner. One of the phrases in the mark scheme that examiners use to assess your performance is 'confident conceptual exploration'. Aim to be able to do this.

Representations

Nothing in the media is real, even something that attempts to give information about a real-life event. Everything in the mass media that is seen, heard or read has been constructed. You, as the consumer of the media, are getting a second-hand experience.

Many media texts give the impression that what they show is realistic, but even the news is **re-presented** to the consumer. The voice and appearance of the newsreader may be familiar and authoritative, and the programme may broadcast pictures from the scene of the event, but the content, style and format of the news package has been constructed, a process which involves selection and editing. Decisions have been made as to what to put in and what to leave out. These decisions are affected by the time available, the accessibility of the news story itself and the choices made by the news producers about what they think is appropriate and interesting for their viewers. You are not seeing the real thing — it has been **mediated** by the very fact that it has been selected and shaped. When considering the concept of represent-ation, you are examining the processes and techniques that shape texts. You must ask the following questions:

- Is the representation fair and accurate?
- What is the purpose of the representation?
- What might the audience make of the representation?
- Is stereotyping used? Why?

Look in detail at the language and form of the text and consider its genre. You need to be able to support your ideas by giving detailed references to the processes by which the representation has been constructed. This will help you to understand how and why the representation was made and how the audience receives it.

Applying the concept

Suppose you are studying different types of broadcast fiction, e.g. soap operas and situation comedies. You are looking particularly at the concept of representation and your text is *My Family*, a popular sitcom which has had several series and is broadcast to a family audience on BBC1. It is about the life of a middle-class family consisting of a professional father and mother and their three children. The setting is usually a domestic one, centring upon various rooms in the comfortable house in which they live. As in most sitcoms, there is a new 'problem' in every programme but the characters and their relationships with each other stay more or less the same throughout the series. There is always conflict between the characters, particularly between the parents and one or other of their children. The humour lies in the misunderstandings and the interaction between the characters — particularly the mother and the father, who remain loving but exasperated by their children.

Imagine that you are examining one 30-minute episode looking particularly at issues of representation. You could look in detail at the representation of any of the following:

- family life
- middle-class, middle-aged marriage
- working women/mothers
- men
- parenting
- teenagers

Look closely at the codes used to construct the characters: what does the unconventional hairstyle of the mother signify? What message does it give the audience about the balance in her life? Note the elements of stereotyping present in the constructions of the children and consider how these factors (endearingly irresponsible, manipulative and boy mad, resourceful and intelligent) add to the humour and often form the basis of the narrative.

Media languages and forms

This concept addresses the ways in which the language (words and sounds, images and shapes) of any media text are 'read' or interpreted by the people who read, view or listen to them. It is concerned with understanding the processes involved in the construction of media texts and how the techniques used in the construction affect the way the message is interpreted by the receiver.

Semiology, the study of signs, is the starting point for studying individual texts and making comparisons between them. The **technical codes** particular to a media form carry with them **cultural meanings**. Examples of this include the size and font of the masthead on a newspaper front page, or the over-the-shoulder shots and spooky music in a dramatic scene from a horror film. You must be able to **denotate** (describe accurately) the detail that makes up the language of a text and **connotate** (say what meaning the language may carry).

One of the most interesting aspects about the media is that the meaning intended by the maker of the media product, the **preferred meaning**, does not always come across. This is because the reader of the text interprets it in the light of previous thoughts, ideas and experiences and may make different cultural connotations. An example of this was when, about 40 years ago, an advertising agency produced a television advertisement for a brand of cigarettes. The main character was standing alone on a city street-corner on a dark and rainy night, wearing a belted raincoat and trilby hat and lighting a cigarette. This was intended to show the brand as sophisticated and the character as an urbane detective, reminiscent of Hollywood films noirs. The majority of television viewers read this another way, and saw the character as seedy and isolated — they gave the cigarettes negative connotations. The brand went out of production. Texts that are open to different interpretations in this way are called **polysemic**.

When considering the concept of media language and forms you must avoid merely describing what is there. You must look at all the elements in the text and explain how they carry cultural meaning.

Applying the concept

To practise your analysis of media language you can interrogate any text from any topic area in this module. Make sure you know the terminology of the moving-image media (e.g. *mise-en-scène*, reaction shots, diagetic sound, montage) and that of the print-based media (e.g. masthead, anchorage, editorial, exclusive). For Modules 1 and 6 you must be familiar with radio, too. Your examination centre will know a few weeks before the exams whether the unseen texts are print, video or audio based. If you are studying film and broadcast fiction, you should make detailed readings of significant parts of specific texts, and be able to explain how the processes involved in constructing the messages shape the meanings and carry the story to audiences, using:

- non-verbal structures (e.g. facial expression, position, gesture, clothing, props)
- sound and visual techniques (e.g. camera positioning, editing, relationship between sounds and images)
- *mise-en-scène*. This refers to the way in which objects, scenery and the location are shown by using light and dark, pattern, colour, camera position and angle, and movement within the frame. *Mise-en-scène* establishes mood and atmosphere and can express the inner life of the characters through the way in which their settings are depicted.

Narrative

Narrative is closely related to media language and is concerned with the form or structure of the text itself, the way it tells the story, and how it is shaped. You will have come across the word 'narrator', meaning story-teller, and the narrative is the story that is told or written. In the context of the mass media the story is the media text and a whole team of people has been involved in creating and shaping it for the consumer. A narrative is present in all media texts.

Narrative is a process of organising and structuring. It is easy to work out the narrative pattern of a fictional text, such as a film, and there are theoretical models which can be used to look at the regular patterns found in film and television drama. These are explained in the film and broadcast section of this guide (pp. 25–29). You should be able to describe the ways in which narrative is constructed in individual texts of any form. Comment on any narrative patterns in the topic you are studying and be able to account for similarities and differences. You need to be able to talk about how the producers control the flow of information and how this affects the way the story is understood by the audience. In newspapers, for example, a large, eye-catching photograph or a dramatic headline is the first part of the story that the reader notices, and may, in fact, be the only part of the story read. These elements therefore form the basis on which the reader's opinion is formed.

There are differences between two texts of the same type. For example, sporting events on television such as a football match have a different narrative structure depending on whether the broadcast is live or whether the producers screen the event later. When the whole event is shown as a live broadcast, the viewers appear to be in the same position as the spectators in the stadium, as they do not yet know the final result.

EastEnders and *Hollyoaks*, and note the shared features of moving image conventions, character, themes and narrative structure. Differences between the two programmes could be accounted for by looking at the audience (different target audiences and different time slots in the television schedule), and institutions responsible (BBC1 and Channel 4 respectively).

Genres develop and evolve with advances in technology, shifts in popular culture and changes in the nature of audiences. Although audiences like familiarity, they also want to be surprised by the unexpected. Producers know how genre works and how to attract audiences with a mixture of the familiar and the surprising.

Genres that are a mixture of existing ones are called **hybrid genres**. If you look at a weekly television listing magazine you will find a number of types of made-for-television drama: medical drama, comedy drama, crime drama, police drama, documentary drama. These are classified in terms of their subject matter, style and conventions to market them to an audience. Genres are not fixed; producers combine aspects of different genres to attract particular audiences.

Sometimes genres are given a playful treatment, and conventions and iconography are used to create a **parody** or **pastiche**. A parody, sometimes referred to as a 'spoof', seeks to make fun of or send up a generic text, whereas a pastiche merely uses, or copies, the stylistic features of the original with no mocking intent.

One way for the film industry to draw a young audience into the cinema has been to use television or popular music performers in acting roles. Stars associated with specific genres have always been important in creating expectations in an audience. When Will Smith was cast in *Independence Day* (1996) he brought aspects of his character from *The Fresh Prince of Bel-Air* to the film, and this was one of the factors that brought a new, young audience to the cinema. Smith's casting was calculated to appeal to females and black people, not the traditional science-fiction audience. The film contained traditional conventions of science fiction, such as eccentric scientists, evil aliens, special effects involving spaceships and war above the earth, but added elements of comedy which brought something new to the genre.

Applying the concept

Work on genre is often film-based and is an important concept in film studies. However, you must question each text you are studying, not just films or television programmes. Consider the ways in which genre works in newspapers, for instance, by looking at readers' expectations, the repetition of features and the balance between the familiar and the unexpected. Similarly, think about genre in relation to advertising. All advertisements share certain conventions — the product, the slogan, the space taken or time-slot — but can be broken down into categories according to the product or service advertised. For example, you could look at adverts for cars and adverts for beer and note the differences between them in style and appeal. Explore how far audience expectations are fulfilled or otherwise and whether the generic conventions are treated playfully by using parody or pastiche.

Audiences

In order for communication to take place, two parties must be involved: the sender and the recipient of the communication. Every media text is produced with an audience in mind. The audience is the receiver of the text and interprets the message conveyed. Without an audience, the message carried by the text would not reach anyone and its meaning would be lost. The concept of audience is closely linked with that of institution: the institutions (media owners and producers) are concerned with making/providing media texts that will reach **target audiences**.

The media institutions spend much time and money on researching audience preferences and building up audience profiles, which guide them in their decisions about which films, television programmes, magazines, newspapers, pop groups and so on to finance.

> **Tip**
> Examine television viewing figures, magazine and newspaper circulation figures, and cinema box office figures to work out which genres are popular with audiences. Ask yourself what the appeal is and why such texts are popular at this point in time.

Quantitative data about audiences are broken down by institutions into demographics (information about age, social class, address, occupation). This can give a detailed picture of which texts appeal to which audiences, and can guide producers towards constructing more of the same, or developing the genre in ways which will maintain the audience's interest.

In the marketing industry, audience research is a vital part of a process that is fundamentally concerned with discovering audience thoughts, feelings, needs and aspirations and creating and/or packaging a product in a way that will deliver it to the audience successfully. Methods of research include questionnaires, interviews and focus groups. Advertisers use the same methods to investigate the effect of advertisements on audiences.

The relationship between the media and their audiences has always been a matter of debate and there have been shifts in ideas about the relative power of the media and the audience. In the early twentieth century, behavioural theorists saw the media as a hypodermic needle, injecting the ideas held by the powerful groups in society into passive individuals. Since then, opinion has shifted, recognising that audiences already have well-developed attitudes, that their identity is formed by the many social groups to which they belong and, most importantly, that they consciously and actively select and interpret messages.

> **Tip**
> Think about how audiences use the media. Many people would say, for example, that they are better able to deal with personal problems by watching soap operas. While continuing to attract audiences with entertaining characters and dramatic narratives,

20-something year-old professionals — what does this say about the perception of the programme-makers regarding the racial mix in New York and the representation of ethnic minorities in the professions? (In reality, white people make up less than half the population of Manhattan.) To understand how institution works in a text it is important to consider the other Key Concepts, particularly representation, audience, values and ideology.

> **Applying the concept**
>
> Institutional factors are a vital part of the information you need for each of the topic areas in Unit 2.
>
> **Film and broadcast fiction** Consider the institutional issues relating to film and broadcast fiction texts: differences within the institutions, for example Hollywood and non-Hollywood film producers; the influence of finance, marketing and distribution upon the production and reception of texts.
>
> **Documentary** Who produces documentaries? How much power does the institution have on the documentary maker? Why are reality TV documentaries popular with the institutions that commission them?
>
> **Advertising and marketing** The advertising and marketing industry is an institution in itself. How powerful is it as a major provider of finance to the media institutions (commercial television companies, magazine and newspaper publishers and film distributors) which deliver audiences to advertisers? How mutually dependent are media institutions?
>
> **British newspapers** Look at press ownership and the connection between the owner's views and the political orientation of the newspaper, the fact that the industry is regulated by its own members, the potential role of British newspapers in forming public opinion about social and cultural issues.

Values and ideology

Values

Attitudes, beliefs and values are terms used to describe our various responses to the world. Our values are our basic responses to reality and are based on the worth we place on aspects of our lives, including events and people. They are the foundation on which we base our behaviour and they are culturally shared. For example, the majority of people in Britain share the view that the best way to bring up children is within the family home by two parents. Although this does not reflect the reality of life in British society, it can be argued that it is the model to which the majority aspires. We experience the world primarily through the family and social groups to which we belong and — from a very early age — through what we read, see and hear in the mass media.

Identify the values carried by the media and the beliefs about society which are **naturalised** within texts. Texts deliver assumptions about life that can affect how their consumers think about themselves and others. For example, in the majority of media texts the predominant image of a female is of an attractive, tall and very slim young woman, often with long, blonde hair. This can be seen as the only desirable appearance for a woman; it has become naturalised or taken for granted.

> **Tip**
>
> To explore this naturalised image of the ideal female, look at a number of media texts and note the proportion of young, tall, slim women in advertisements in newspapers, magazines, outdoor advertising (including bill-boards, buses and taxis etc.) and at the cinema as well as on news programmes, in film and broadcast fiction and documentary programmes. What message does this send to women about what they think they should look like, and how could this affect their aspirations, thoughts and behaviour? Why is this 'ideal woman' so prevalent? You will find that there are far fewer representations of women who have different body shapes. Why has this image of women become naturalised rather than other images?

Our view of the world is filtered through the media. The media have a powerful role in reinforcing or changing our attitudes towards events and people, and can sometimes provoke action. The *News of The World* started a 'naming and shaming' campaign by publishing the names and addresses of paedophiles, some of which were incorrect. The newspaper gained publicity and extra sales and unleashed vigilante behaviour. It was accused of generating a moral panic. The *Daily Mirror* ran an anti-war campaign in March 2003, which encouraged readers to demonstrate against war in Iraq. The paper even provided a cut-out poster for readers to put in their windows. This poster indicated that the reader shared the *Daily Mirror*'s views and the paper's name was visible to the onlooker, thus promoting it as being serious-minded and having a social conscience. The editorial and opinion sections of tabloid and broadsheet newspapers are often revealing, as they may encourage their readers to adopt a particular attitude towards a political, social or national issue.

Ideology

Ideology is a set of beliefs that people use to make sense of their experiences and views of the world. The most obvious belief systems centre upon religious, political and economic concepts. The construction, selection and shaping of ideas that go into a media text can be seen to reflect the belief system of the originator of the text.

Historically, the people who ran the media institutions shared the same narrow social class and educational background as those who made up the higher ranks of government, the legal profession and the civil service, and were therefore likely to share the same values. These people were mostly white, middle class and educated at public schools and Oxbridge. The same ideology (attitudes, beliefs and values) was seen across the majority of media and was implicit in every medium, resulting in a state of **hegemony**. Hegemony is the domination of a powerful professional elite which imposes a certain worldview on the rest of the population in order to maintain the status quo, i.e. the situation in which the elite's views about religion, politics,

Narratives

Narratives are shaped differently in film and broadcast texts and a number of narrative techniques or devices are used by producers and enjoyed by audiences. A variety of ideas can be applied when looking at the narrative structure of film and broadcast fiction texts. Some focus on how a fairly harmonious situation is disrupted by some sort of conflict, with an event or character sometimes being the agent of change. The story may continue with a series of dramatic events until finally harmony is re-established, the problem is solved and the conflict is over. Narratives can be examined in terms of the roles that characters play in the story, too: the clash of opposites, e.g. the forces of good and evil, red-neck country people and sophisticated city dwellers, warring political factions. A useful way of looking at how the narrative progresses in a story is to consider enigma and action codes. The work of Roland Barthes, a French cultural theorist, examined how certain devices draw the reader (or, in the case of a film or broadcast text, the viewer) into the progress of the story. Action codes can work as a shorthand way of advancing the narrative. We see or hear something and know what is going to happen. We are familiar with signifiers, such as a girl being alone in the house when the telephone rings, and have the pleasure of anticipation as to what might happen. The enigma code is a narrative device which captures audiences by involving them in a puzzle that they want to see solved. Audiences enjoy predicting the outcome of a particular narrative.

You should be aware of the overall narrative structure of the films and broadcast fiction texts you study, but the first 10 minutes or so of a fiction text are particularly important for setting up the story and engaging the audience in the narrative. The ending scenes are important too and you should study these in some detail.

There are differences between the closed endings of most films and plays (texts which are often 90–120 minutes long) and the open ending of each episode in a soap opera. Consider too how the different conditions of viewing for a cinema or television audience might explain this. The cliff-hanger endings and ongoing storylines in soap operas keep the viewer keen to watch the next episode, while the definite resolution of a film narrative leaves the audience satisfied. Some texts have a single narrative and others have several story-lines. Some are linear and others use techniques such as **flashback** or **flashforward**. Be aware of these differences and the reasons for them.

Look closely at characters and the role certain characters play in particular narratives. Actors are another important aspect, as particular people carry narrative expectations to audiences. Audiences might expect a film starring Hugh Grant to be a light-hearted romantic comedy because of his roles in *Four Weddings and a Funeral* (1994) and *Notting Hill* (1999). His name carries narrative expectation. However, narrative expectations might be upset when a comic actor, e.g. Robin Williams, plays a disturbing character, as was the case in *One Hour Photo* (2002).

Tip

Narrative techniques relate closely to genre in terms of conventions of narrative, characters, iconography and moving image techniques. Narrative structures and the ways that characters work in fiction can be examined via the work of theorists, but there is no substitute for careful textual analysis to understand how the form of each text is shaped to carry the story.

Representation

Look at how individuals, groups, places and ideas are represented in film and broadcast fiction texts. Examine the construction of these representations, how they are conveyed by the media language, and their role in the narrative. Are these fair and accurate, and should they be? Groups are represented and received in different ways according to the types of text in which they appear. For example, producers might portray teenagers differently in a sitcom such as *My Family* and a police drama such as *The Bill*. Think about the relationship these representations may have with their audiences, especially if they are stereotypes. Consider their purpose in the specific texts you study, and think about which individuals are not represented in the text and why this is so. For example, *EastEnders* has a range of middle-aged and female characters whereas *Hollyoaks* has a range of young adults. In this case the genre is the same, but the programme is targeted at a different audience, and espouses different values and ideology.

Tip
You need to be able to express your views about the ideas above and support them with examples of representations. You may have studied some theories of representation which you can use to evaluate the representations in the texts you have studied.

Audience

Media texts are produced with audiences in mind, and films and broadcast fiction texts can appeal to a wide or a narrow audience. You may have studied radio fiction, and might know that the Radio 4 soap opera *The Archers*, which is broadcast daily with an omnibus on Sundays, has a far larger audience than the daily afternoon play on the same station. For all the texts you study, decide who the people are that make up the target audience, how they might 'read' the text, and how and why they engage with the characters, story and themes.

Some television fiction deals with social problems and domestic conflicts which are present in society and with which audiences can identify. What does the target audience bring to the text? What does it get out of the text? Examine the text itself in detail and consider the scheduling of television programmes, and the genre and distribution of films. Some texts are targeted at a niche audience and may not be seen widely. For example, a film may offer an ideology that is not widely shared, characters who do not appeal to mass audiences, and ideas and scenes which are considered to be unsuitable for some audiences. The US film *Kids** (1995), for example, upset traditional and conservative views and was not distributed widely. Alternatively, they may simply be made in a language other than English. *Belleville Rendez-vous* (2003),

is evidence of bias involved and just how much reality is present. Documentaries can be biased, particularly when the director chooses which angle to take on the subject — these are sometimes referred to as 'director is king' documentaries.

Editing is a way of interpreting an event into a comprehensible form. It shapes the audience's understanding of what is represented. The post-production conventions of constructing a narrative involve an editorial process of selecting certain shots from a range of material, compressing certain material, perhaps adding an authoritative voice-over and a music track to interpret events and anchor the images, and often simplifying or dramatising aspects of the subject. The effect of the camera and the crew must be considered when assessing apparently realistic events and interactions; situations being set up, repeated or reconstructed for the camera all impact on the impression of spontaneity and naturalism which documentaries may seek to give. To meet the perceived requirements of the institution or audience, the documentary may be intended to function as entertainment. You should be able to illustrate the use of techniques and how they mediate the 'real world', and to discuss how the representation of reality is constructed.

Style and content

Think about the links between the style of the documentary and its content. Documentaries are made about different subjects and for different purposes, and the style chosen by the documentary maker reflects this. Examine different types of documentary and compare the ways in which content is presented. You should be able to identify the different forms of documentary according to their function. There are many ways of classifying documentary forms — do not focus on learning their labels but on analysing how the stylistic elements used are appropriate.

Expository documentaries

Most early documentaries took the expository form and it is still commonly used. This type of documentary aims to inform and educate, usually addressing a topic with which the audience is not familiar. The script, delivered by voice-over (often referred to as the 'voice of God'), explains the accompanying images to the audience. The script is the means whereby images are selected, shaped and delivered to the viewer. Wildlife programmes, historical documentaries and science documentaries follow this tradition.

Observational documentaries

The observational mode of documentary stems from direct cinema and cinéma vérité. These documentaries do not attempt to interpret their subject by the use of a voice-over but instead let events unfold before the cameras. This format is characterised by hand-held cameras and a lack of staging and extra lighting. Documentaries which can be loosely classified as observational include fly-on-the-wall programmes, undercover/investigatory texts and docu-soaps. There is constant development within this rather loose genre and contemporary observational formats often include participants addressing the camera and interacting with the programme makers.

Reflexive documentaries

The reflexive mode of documentary is generally one in which the documentary maker has some part to play. He or she interacts with the subject of the documentary in some way, perhaps to create a special perspective. Examples of this include Louis Theroux, who seems innocent and naïve, and Michael Moore, who is interventionist. The documentary maker may be in the visual and/or sound frame. Documentaries which are authored in this way show you something of the person who made them as well as the subject matter of the piece.

The positive values of documentary

Documentaries fulfil a variety of functions and provide valuable sources of information, education and illumination about historical, geographical, scientific, artistic and social subject matter. They can present a case, highlight an injustice and give a voice to issues which may not otherwise be aired. Documentaries can have a campaigning role and some are designed to provoke thought and action from their audiences. They can be controversial and inspire public debate. For example, the BBC documentary *The Secret Policeman* exposed racism among police recruits. As a result a number of officers resigned and changes to the police training system were devised.

The development of the documentary

You need to study some early documentaries in order to understand how the medium has changed. Developments in technology have had a profound effect. Early documentary-makers had heavy equipment and poor sound recording facilities, which affected what could be filmed and how they filmed it. The availability of light, hand-held 16 mm film cameras in the 1960s made it possible for documentary makers to film more easily and without obstructing the action to such an extent. Since then, video cameras have become widely available and easy to use and this has led to members of the public being able to make their own filmed records of events, which have been broadcast as video diaries. Ordinary people can make documentaries, and ordinary people can appear in them. There has been a development in the public's access to the production process, with a greater chance for people to have their say. You need to be able to compare two documentaries in some detail and should choose texts which use different techniques and have been made for different purposes by different documentary makers.

Docu-soaps became very popular with audiences and producers in the 1990s. The public enjoyed getting to know 'ordinary' people, and going behind the scenes at a hotel or an airport, for example. This format is a hybrid of the expository and observational modes. Producers of docu-soaps select people on the basis of their personalities, and the programmes focus on how they deal with dramatic situations. Reality TV programmes, which select 'ordinary' people and put them into artificial situations, can be regarded as a form of documentary because events unfold before the camera.

industry and have a clear knowledge and understanding of covert techniques, such as sponsorship and public relations, which are not paid for in terms of time or space. You must be able to refer to details of each of these strategies and comment on how they address their audience, which necessitates studying each text closely.

Advertising

Advertisements can consist of visual images, sound or written text, or any combination of these. Most advertisements are short and can be analysed in detail through the process of denotation and connotation. Always consider the technical codes chosen and how each element of the text works with the other elements to suggest certain promises and values about the product to its target audience. Study the tactics and techniques that advertising and marketing strategies use to gain attention. Devices such as humour, repetition, shock tactics, sex, music and influential or famous people are often used for this purpose. The format of the advertisement should be considered too — look at whether the product is at the centre of all the other elements on display, or whether the format gives the product an image which is associated with a certain lifestyle.

> **Tip**
> Popular campaigns often include amusing characters, a catchy slogan, attention-grabbing activity, or a continuing story. What is original and interesting about current advertisements? You need to evaluate the campaign or promotional techniques you have studied.

Advertising techniques

Advertisers use a variety of techniques, both promotional and covert. They range from sponsorship and product placement to public relations and 'plugs' in the media, and the industry is constantly developing new techniques to reach audiences. We live in a promotional culture in which institutions compete against each other. For example, universities promote themselves to potential students and will have a stall at a careers fair — they might give you a free pen as you pass by. Some financial institutions, such as Lloyds TSB, offer hospitality at sporting events such as the Wimbledon Lawn Tennis Championship in order to associate themselves with all that is English and traditional. People can be less resistant to subtle methods such as these than they are to direct advertising. Covert strategies can be less expensive, too, although creating an impact still costs money.

You need to study a range of covert techniques and evaluate what they are trying to do and why they, rather than other methods, are used. Don't simply produce a list of techniques; use the conceptual framework to explore the connections between the product, the text and the target audience as fully as you can. Make sure you understand the differences between advertisements that are paid for according to the time or space they take up in the media and strategies which cannot be accounted for in the same way. For example, when sports stars appear in television advertisements for trainers, both they and the television channel are paid — this is overt advertising in which the athletes endorse the product commercially. However, when a sports star wearing a brand of sunglasses is photographed by the press, the manufacturer of the glasses has not paid the photographer or paid for news space, but still gains publicity and association with the glamour of the occasion. This is covert advertising. The sports star gains publicity which adds to his or her commercial worth and may have been given the sunglasses or been paid to wear them rather than another brand.

Intextuality is an important area to study here. Think about the links between a media text and its sponsor, for instance Daz and *Emmerdale*. Why do certain products, such as sports cars and expensive watches, appear in James Bond films? Consider the special significance of tie-ins such as giving away toys based on a current Disney film with McDonald's meals. Consider what L'Oréal, Nescafé or Jacob's Creek wine say about *Friends* and vice versa, and what these products and the programme say about Channel 4.

Marketing

Marketing is a term that has changed its meaning during the twentieth century. When it first appeared in a commercial context it meant selling standardised goods at the lowest price, and was producer-driven rather than customer-centred as it is today. This type of minimum-choice marketing is expressed in the phrase attributed to Henry Ford about the colour options for the Ford Model-T: 'They can have any colour they want so long as it's black.' Today marketeers are responsible for identifying, anticipating and satisfying consumer requirements. Marketing is people-led and not product-led. Finding out what people might want, accept and believe is at the root of marketing. Products are promoted in such a way as to offer the promise of satisfying customer needs and aspirations. There is a difference between marketing and selling, and a principle of marketing philosophy is that consumers have freedom of choice. Market research is used to find out which groups make up the marketplace and how these groups see themselves. You will have learned the ways in which audiences can be categorised into a variety of social groups according to factors such as social class, psychographics, demographics and lifestyle types. These classifications draw on sociological, psychological and economic theories about society, and some are referred to by the industry by acronyms, e.g. DINKY (double income, no kids yet), or by labels to describe attitude to life, e.g. pleasure-seekers or achievers. You can find out about the most recent terminology from the Advertising Association, and if you contact the agencies involved in your campaign case study you may get some specific information about how they identify the target audience. Market researchers use questionnaires, surveys, focus groups, previews and other events to find out what different groups believe in or aspire to. Other aspects of marketing involve product design, product testing and evaluation, pricing, production and distribution. Remember that there are differences in how marketing is approached in business studies and how it relates to media studies. The media studies angle focuses on the Key Concepts, in this case language, representation, audience, institution and ideology.

> **Tip**
>
> Always link any theories or information about marketing and advertising to your analysis and evaluation of the texts and campaigns themselves. Merely repeating second-hand learned material does not demonstrate your media studies skills.

Branding

Branding is a marketing practice which seeks to show a product, person or idea as being both special and different from its competitors; it has a special mark or brand which makes it stand out, offers a guarantee of value and suggests some form of promise. A pair of trainers, a holiday in Ibiza, a new teen band or an idea, such as the family Christmas, can deliver promises through emotional association. Marketeers work on establishing and positioning a brand and sometimes have to engage in rebranding when a brand has lost its appeal. Some people are almost a brand in themselves and carry a wealth of associations, e.g. David Beckham, Richard Branson and Madonna.

Branding can be seen most easily when comparing different forms of the same product. For example, how does the brand image differ between Coca-Cola and Pepsi or between Nike and Adidas? You may have brand loyalty to a particular drink or make of trainers. What does this say about the product and what does it say about you? Think about how a brand has a particular image and how it is different from other brands. Consider the importance of branding to institutions and audiences; you could look at the BBC brand — what it means and how it is conveyed in texts.

Funding

Advertising is not a medium itself. It is connected with other media and provides a large proportion of the funds which enable media texts to be produced, as well as buying advertising space on television, cinema and outdoor advertising. This extends to advertorials (advertising material presented as an article) in newspapers and magazines, and product placement in films and some television programmes.

The question of funding raises ethical debates on the potential influence of funding on programme makers who need to raise money for production costs. How far can advertisers tell directors and writers what should or should not be included? Another side of this debate is the media's need to fill air-time on the increasing number of television, radio, print and internet outlets. The objectivity of reporters can be called into question if, for example, they are treated to a free holiday and subsequently write an article for newspaper travel pages which also contain direct advertisements for the country and even for airlines and hotels concerned. The paper needs copy and the tourist destination needs publicity. Think about how public service broadcasters indirectly promote commercial interests in 'factual' programmes about houses, gardens and cooking. How many institutions benefit from chat-show appearances, newspaper and radio interviews and news coverage of a Hollywood film premiere? How often does an item on a broadcast news programme promote the station's own programmes?

Politics and marketing

Political parties, figures and issues are all subject to marketing. Promotional tactics are an important part of the ways in which the government and other institutions communicate with the public. Political parties and leaders appoint press officers, sometimes called 'spin doctors', who attempt to manage the way a story or issue is interpreted by the media, so that a story is told in such a way that it works to their advantage and shows events in a favourable light. Politicians, members of the royal family and others attempt to influence the presentation of stories about them in order to convey or protect a specific image. The principles and practice of branding and re-branding to offer an image, a promise and a value applies as much to people and ideas as it does to soap powder. From August to October 2003 the Hutton enquiry investigated whether the government or the civil service had exaggerated a claim about the capability of Iraq's weapons of mass destruction in order to influence public opinion to support Britain's involvement in the Iraq war. A BBC reporter attempted to expose the source of the exaggeration and was questioned as part of the enquiry. All of the news media were engaged in looking at the BBC's relationship with government 'spin'.

> **Tip**
>
> Keep up to date even when you have 'finished' studying the topic. Take note of occasions when advertising or marketing campaigns become the subject of media reports in the newspapers and on television and look carefully at those texts or events that have captured media attention. Visit the Advertising Standards Authority's website (**www.asa.org.uk**) to see which advertisements it has received complaints about and why. The Advertising Association's website (**www.adassoc.org.uk**) is a useful reference for developments in the industry. Think about public relations and promotional activities. For example, why did Cherie Blair allow *Marie Claire* photographers into her house for the September 2003 edition? What image did she present of herself amid her young child's toys and how does this magazine coverage affect the country's attitude to her, her husband and the Labour government?

British newspapers

You should have built up some solid knowledge about the newspaper industry in Britain, including how the press is regulated and criticisms of the way in which it operates. You need to be able to discuss the range of newspapers available, be aware of their similarities and differences and be able to give reasons for these. You should also make a detailed study of at least two newspapers which you read over a period of time. One of these should be a tabloid newspaper and the other a broadsheet. You should be familiar with a local newspaper too. You need to be aware of the ways news is gathered, selected and presented and to make a close study of specific newspapers and particular stories and features that are noteworthy and/or typical.

Analysing and evaluating newspapers

Newspapers can be categorised in the following ways:

- size and type (tabloid and broadsheet)
- content and readership (up market, middle market or down market)
- production and readership (national morning daily, local morning daily, local weekly, free newspaper)
- ownership and/or political bias

All newspapers have their own identities which are expressed through a combination of design, content and language. Media language analysis should cover:

- design and layout
- typeface
- masthead
- images used (cropping, framing, camera angle/shot etc.)
- captions
- use and type of headlines
- formality or otherwise of language used

These elements can be seen by comparing the front pages of tabloid newspapers and broadsheet newspapers. What do the masthead and title of the newspaper signify? How do they achieve this? How does the layout help to attract readers and what impression or message is given out by the overall 'look' of the front page?

You must, however, look beyond the front pages of the newspapers you choose for your case study. You should notice, and be able to discuss, the significance of by-lines, exclusives, promotions, the difference between news and features, and the amount and type of display and classified advertising. Don't forget to study the editorial/opinion sections of the newspapers. There is a marked contrast between the journalistic styles used in tabloids and broadsheet evident in the use of puns, the way readers are addressed, and the tone of the stories and articles — these stylistic features need careful scrutiny. See if you can identify a house style. Having looked at several print editions of each newspaper, compare them with the online version and account for any differences you observe.

Follow a particular story as it happens, over a few days or weeks, perhaps a trial, a crime, a war, a scandal, or follow the longer term, more occasional coverage of issues such as the euro or asylum seekers. You could study the coverage of a local issue, for example people's opinions about a new road, in your local paper. Keep cuttings from more than one newspaper and compare the treatment of facts, the vocabulary used, the tone of the writing and the view held by the writer. Relate this to the newspaper concerned, its values and ideology, its readership and its need to sell issues.

Tip

Be aware of breaking news and be prepared to buy several newspapers of different types or different political persuasions. You can obtain back copies or read articles online if you miss an edition.

Criticisms of the British press

The British press is known as a free press and is not subject to regulation by law, except the laws relating to libel and slander. The Press Complaints Commission, which was set up in 1991, is made up largely of editors who have worked in the industry and considers complaints against the press. There is an ongoing debate between the newspaper owners and editors and some members of the government and the public as to whether legislation should be put in place to control some aspects of press coverage. The British press is a changing medium and the situation regarding control and regulation is a fluid one. You cannot rely on textbooks for up-to-the-minute information.

> **Tip**
>
> Read the papers, listen to the news, ask at the library and use the internet to keep up-to-date. This applies to facts about press ownership and the political stance of particular newspapers too. The media section of the *Guardian* on Mondays is a useful resource for issues about the press.

The criticisms levelled against the press, and particularly the tabloids, are those of invasion of privacy, sensationalism, inaccuracy and fabrication, entrapment and propaganda. There are also cases of 'chequebook journalism', where newspapers compete to buy a person's story. There have even been cases where newspaper reports, for example during a trial, have interfered with the processes of the law. During the trial of some Leeds footballers accused of an assault outside a nightclub, a Sunday newspaper published an interview with a relative of one of the injured parties. The jury was dismissed and the case had to go to re-trial.

Celebrities, including members of the royal family, have sought injunctions against the British press to stop the publication of articles and photographs. The editors of the newspapers concerned offer the defence that the story is in the public interest; perhaps it was exposing crime or a serious misdemeanour, protecting public health and safety, or preventing the public from being misled. However, it could be argued that it was, equally, in the interest of newspaper sales. Sections of the tabloid press have been accused of setting up stories, for example the kidnap attempt on Victoria Beckham. A general criticism levelled particularly at the tabloid papers is that the content is overly concerned with gossip and scandal, and focuses on the world of show business at the expense of more serious national and international events and issues.

> **Tip**
>
> Consider whether these criticisms are valid and find evidence to support your views from current newspaper content. Read what newspapers say about other newspapers. Some newspapers compete against others for the same audience and this can lead to writing negatively about their rivals, e.g. the *Sun* and the *Daily Mirror* or the *Daily Mail* and the *Daily Express*.

What purpose and functions do newspapers serve and why do people read them? What part do they play in readers' lives? Your analysis of a tabloid, a broadsheet and a local paper will reveal how information, entertainment and opinions are presented.

Newspapers cater to a range of their readers' interests. Daily broadsheet newspapers offer detailed coverage of national and international news, columnists using a range of styles who provide opinions and insights into contemporary life, reviews of new books, films and events, specialist supplements giving detailed information and opinion about such things as education, sport, science, travel, finance and jobs. Tabloids have similar features, providing information and gossip tailored to their particular target audience. Readers enjoy the focus on celebrities and other well-known people and relish the scandals that are often featured in such papers. Headlines and captions in newspapers, particularly tabloids, are witty and provide amusement for their readers. Online newspapers keep readers updated on breaking news and provide the opportunity to access the archives for stories.

The press is not controlled by any government agency, and journalists and editors see it as their civic duty to investigate and bring to light issues that they think the public should know about, matters that are considered to be in the public interest. Investigative journalism is a strength in the British press and there is a tradition of uncovering fraud and corruption in business and politics. In 2003 Michael Crick's investigations contributed to the replacement of Iain Duncan Smith as leader of the Conservative Party.

Some newspapers encourage readers to interact with the newspaper by expressing an opinion or voting on an issue, and local newspapers attempt to construct a sense of community, often including reports from members of the public. Do newspapers give people what they want, fulfilling specific needs? Do newspapers influence their readers? At election time, for example, newspapers give views which favour one party over another.

Tip
Find detailed, up-to-date examples to support your views on the positive and negative aspects of the press.

Ideology and values

The British press is privately owned. Historically, rich businessmen bought newspapers and used them to express their opinions and to attempt to influence public opinion. You should be able to provide evidence, from newspaper headlines, articles and editorials, of any paper's political views. A number of newspapers express politically, economically or socially biased views but, unlike broadcasting institutions, there is no requirement for them to present a balanced view to their audience. At the moment News International has the largest share of British newspapers and the anti-European views of Rupert Murdoch, its owner, are reflected in the *Sun* and *The Times* when subjects such as Britain adopting the euro are covered.

Most readers choose papers that reflect their views or interests. However, the political leanings of a paper may change, as the *Sun*'s did in 1997, when it shifted its allegiance from the Conservative Party to the Labour Party. Views and attitudes towards social groups and institutions should be the subject of study too, for example the attitudes expressed by different newspapers about football fans, asylum seekers, the Muslim world, women and ethnic minority groups. These issues can be examined by detailed content and textual analysis and also by considering news sources, newsgathering and the editorial processes.

Newspapers are said to operate a system of news and entertainment values which differ between newspapers. News stories are divided into two broad categories which can be loosely classified as 'hard' or 'soft'. **Hard news** is primarily concerned with facts and information and **soft news** covers less substantial or less serious items, such as entertainment. However, you could argue that much of newspaper content is speculation, covering possible future events instead of ones that have already happened. A major influence in the process of **gatekeeping** (deciding what will be included and what excluded) is whether the information is of interest to the audience, or can be presented in such a way as to be interesting. The news values relating to 'hard' news can be classified in the following ways:

- **negativity:** a dramatic or disastrous incident always has a dramatic impact on the audience
- **closeness to home:** readers are more interested in events that happen in their own country than in other places around the world
- **recency:** news media are keen to report a story first, getting a 'scoop' before anyone else discovers the story or covering it from a different angle
- **currency:** a story should be relevant in some way to current ideas or issues that concern the audience
- **continuity:** stories that will run for some time and that have narrative development
- **simplicity:** stories that are easily understood by readers take precedence over stories that are complex and need explanation
- **personality:** the 'human interest' angle which can be centred on a celebrity or an ordinary person

Tip

Examine individual newspapers over a period of time and identify which news values are operating and why. Tabloid newspapers include many stories and features that provide entertainment for their readers, often about the entertainment industries, but all newspapers, even the most serious broadsheets, aim to entertain their readers in the content of the paper and the use of journalistic humour.

Readership

You will be considering audience at every stage of your study of the texts and should try to build up a clear picture of what type of reader is addressed by the content, style and format of each newspaper. A detailed reading of a whole newspaper, including the advertisements and the television selection, should help you to work out what the readership might be. However, a newspaper does not just aim at one type of reader, and not every reader reads the whole paper. Beware of labelling the audience by using simplistic stereotypes such as 'the readers of the *Daily Telegraph* are businessmen' or '*Mirror* readers are working-class, poorly educated, Northern males'. Remember to consider how the newspapers are consumed by audiences.

You can discover what newspapers think of their readers by looking at their media packs which you may be able to get from their advertising departments. Circulation figures for newspapers are published monthly and can be accessed easily. Newspapers attempt to increase their readership by using a variety of tactics, including price-cutting, coupon collecting for special offers and giving away free newspapers in hotels and on trains.

Tip

Don't forget to consider the likely readers of online newspapers, which provide updates on breaking stories on a 24-hour basis and can deliver summaries tailored to individuals.

Questions
&
Answers

This section of the guide provides you with five essay questions of the type you will encounter in the Unit 2 Textual Topics in Contemporary Media exam. Each one is followed by a grade-A and a grade-C answer. Two questions are given for the film and broadcast fiction topic to give you a fuller experience of the case studies, topic ideas and debates that can be used in this broad area. The other four questions are followed by advice about other types of question and how to approach them.

Use these answers as a guide to the structure and style of your essays in terms of relevance to the question, appropriateness of textual detail, coverage of the Key Concepts and reference to topic ideas, debates and theories. The grade-A answers are not model answers in terms of their content, as each candidate will have used different case studies, applied different theories and know different topic information. The content you will use is what you have studied during your course.

At the end of this section are some further examples of exam questions on each topic that you can use to practise writing timed essays.

Examiner's comments

Each answer is accompanied by examiner's comments, preceded by the symbol 🄴. These point out what is creditable within the answers and where answers could be improved. At the end of each answer the examiner explains why the grade would be awarded. Read these comments carefully and pay attention to the strengths and weaknesses that are identified.

Film and broadcast fiction (I)

Present a detailed reading of one film or one broadcast fiction text, and explain its appeal to you and the pleasures it offers to its audience.

■ ■ ■

Grade-A answer

In recent years there have been many television series aimed at the youth market that combine elements of the entertainment values of big-budget films with the day-to-day troubles of teenage life, such as *Roswell*, *Smallville* and the most successful of all of these, *Buffy the Vampire Slayer*. A cinema film of the same name was released in 1992 but it had limited appeal, did not do well at the box office and became nothing more than a 'bargain basement' video. However, it was thought that it still had potential appeal, and the first television series reached cult status in America before coming to England, where it met with much the same result. It has been very popular on BBC2, broadcast in the early-evening slot, and aimed at young adults who do not watch the news programmes offered by the other terrestrial channels at that time.

e This is a sound introductory paragraph which locates the chosen text within its audience and institutional context.

Its success can be attributed to various factors. First, the characters appeal to the target audience. The programme is probably more attractive to girls, but boys enjoy it too, for a variety of reasons. Buffy, played by Sarah Michelle Gellar — an actress already associated with such successful films as *I Know What You Did Last Summer** (1997) — is much like any typical girl in high school, facing all the things every teenager has to face, though on top of this she is the only person who can help stop the world being destroyed by demons and evil gods. Her closest friend Xander (a comical character who often provides mood-lightening one-liners) and Willow (the studious and somewhat unpopular yet likeable character) are all part of the appeal of *Buffy* as a series. These characters each have different roles to play and their actions, words and relationships provide a range of pleasures for the audience. The characters seem to offer companionship with those who watch, as the audience is able to relate to what the characters are going through in their everyday lives. This can be related to Maslow's hierarchy of needs theory, in that an audience seeks companionship through the character on screen. For the teenage audience, friendship and identification with friendship groups is particularly important.

e This paragraph shows detailed knowledge of the main characters and focuses on the question by referring to the appeal of a known actress for audiences and the pleasures offered by a range of character functions. The reference to and explanation of an appropriate theory is incorporated well and clearly understood. The candidate keeps to the question without digressing.

One of the other reasons *Buffy* continues to appeal to its audience is the issues it deals with and the ideologies behind them. Issues previously addressed by the show include the satanic murder of two children, which turns the town's parents into a crowd of vigilante witch-hunters, leading to an examination of the natural law of trust between parent and child. Themes such as women being powerful and not needing to be rescued by a typical male hero reflect the time of its first release, when the Spice Girls were topping the charts and women felt increasingly independent. These issues relate to the audience, mostly young females living at home with their parents. The ideology behind the show as a whole is that the monsters and demons are metaphors for the problems faced during adolescence, and no matter how many you overcome you will be faced by a new one almost immediately. This reflects the experience of its audience but dramatises these battles using the iconography of the vampire/horror genre, which is popular with young cinema audiences. In one *Buffy* episode a scene takes place in a graveyard at night, dead people arise from the graves, a high-angle shot (from the point of view of the vampire) shows the potential female victim as vulnerable, but Buffy is able to conquer and kill the vampires. There is a conventional tracking shot through the graveyard, a cut to show the moon and Buffy accompanied by the sound of an owl hooting.

> *e* The candidate develops the discussion to include themes, ideology and genre, thus showing confidence in applying the conceptual framework to the text studied. The use of the term 'iconography' and the detailed illustration of the moving image language of the genre fulfils the question's request for a 'detailed reading'.

The way in which *Buffy* is filmed adds to its appeal too. It is a stylish programme that plays with conventions in ways that appeal to its audience but at the same time keeps viewers enthralled in its story. In the episode 'The Body' we are constantly led to a conclusion about what is happening on screen, and then we are faced with something that catches us completely by surprise. In this episode, the storyline concentrates on the protagonist's mother who dies of a brain tumour. It is only in the final few scenes that we are faced with a vampire, which catches us by surprise. It could be argued that if the episode was to have no paranormal activity or no comic relief it could risk alienating the audience, and if a first-time viewer were to watch the episode, it would not make the same impression as one of the more 'typical' episodes. Like many programmes of this type, several episodes have both an open narrative and a discrete narrative operating at the same time. This makes it much more accessible as first-time viewers are not confused by information that can only be gained from previous knowledge of the show.

> *e* The candidate continues the discussion of *Buffy* using a successful illustration from the text that shows how the programme plays with the narrative conventions of the drama series genre. The use of appropriate terminology, such as 'open narrative' and 'discrete narrative', indicates a good understanding of the concept.

The 14–24-year-old audience is able to get something back from watching *Buffy*, too: there is an element of counter-culture pleasure in the killing of demons. Pleasure can be found too in the glorified action sequences which have elements of computer games or the Gothic counter-culture. In addition, audience gratification is achieved when *Buffy* overcomes her demons as those watching feel like they have overcome them with her. Overall, *Buffy* has retained its audience appeal by facing real-life issues, using modern film techniques and playing with conventions to keep its audience involved and entertained. It offers its audience a chance to escape from reality while still being firmly based in current youth culture. As such it will keep its appeal for some time to come.

 This excellent conclusion sums up the argument and, more importantly, adds the sophisticated notion that the appeal of the text is in escapist and violent fantasy that can be used as a psychological aid.

 This is a sound answer which has all the qualities of a confident conceptual exploration. There is a good understanding of relevant ideas, theories and debates. Note that *Buffy* is a drama series and the candidate refers not only to the appeal of the series as a whole but also to specific episodes, thus presenting the *detailed* reading required by the question. This essay just enters the band for a grade A. With more illustration of the language of the moving image the answer would gain even more marks.

Grade-C answer

The Bone Collector (1999) is part of a sub-genre, initiated by *Se7en** in the 1990s, which has been categorised as 'psychological horror'. *The Bone Collector* tells the story of Lincoln Rhyme, a retired forensics detective who became quadriplegic after a near-fatal accident. As he planned the 'final solution' (euthanasia) he was handed an intriguing case in which a couple were slaughtered after getting a lift home in a New York cab. With the help of Amelia Donaghy, a New York police officer, Lincoln goes in search of the killer through the intricate trail of clues left behind by the murderer.

 The candidate spells out the genre of the film, but the plot summary does not refer to the generic conventions of psychological horrors. The introduction misses a chance to use the conceptual framework fully.

This film appeals to me as it enables the viewer to be involved in the text and solve the enigmas left by the murderer. Barthes's enigma code, whereby a puzzle within the film/text has to be solved, is relevant here. The clues left by the body of the first victim included an iron bolt, oyster shells, a piece of paper with a date and time circled and a woman's wedding ring forced onto the victim's finger. The enigma code highlights the initiation of a puzzle, and this is how Lincoln solved it: the iron bolt was removed from steam pipes; the oyster shells were used as landfill, connoting that the victim was underground; the date and time circled was the point at which the first victim's wife would be killed, denoted by the forcing of the wedding ring onto the victim's finger.

question

> *e* The candidate demonstrates an understanding of enigma and the reference to
> Barthes shows awareness of theory. The explanation of how the enigma is solved
> is descriptive rather than giving a detailed reading of the text. There is a focus on
> the question, as the paragraph outlines what appeals to the candidate personally,
> but this is not developed to cover an audience generally.

An important idea behind the text is 'destiny is what you make it'. Consumed by self-pity, Lincoln feels that his only option is to end his life; however, being involved in the case and building a close relationship with Amelia show that although he is unable to walk there are other aspects of life to be enjoyed. His story enables escapism for the reader, and makes our problems seem all the more pitiful in comparison.

> *e* The ideology of the film is explained with examples and there is a reference to the
> appeal of the message to the audience. This could have been explored further in
> terms of Hollywood film ideology and its relation to the reality of contemporary life.

Another aspect within the text is the use of cinematography to promote dramatic sequences. For example, when Amelia is trying to think of the significance of the number 24799, the use of dramatic music and the contrast between close-ups of Amelia's eyes and black and white images portrayed at a high frequency, maximise the drama of the situation.

> *e* The candidate begins to talk about the film as a piece of cinema rather than a story
> in print format and gives a reasonably detailed example of how the language of the
> moving image works. The point could have been developed into a discussion of the
> appeal to the audience of such conventions. The question calls for a detailed
> reading of one text, so this answer needs more textual analysis.

The use of comedy is important, with the use of 'loud-mouth' expressive characters such as Eddie Ortiz and Paulie Sellitto giving a more light-hearted approach to the film, enabling the audience to take a break from the dramatic conventions of a 'psychological' thriller.

> *e* The audience appeal of light-hearted moments and comedy is implied here but not
> developed fully. The candidate thinks that dramatic conventions have been
> explained, but the answer so far has not shown enough evidence of this.

The cast of the film was also an important element of my enjoyment, with Denzel Washington and Angelina Jolie providing the portrayal of the main characters — Lincoln and Amelia — in superb style. Their portrayal of their relationship provides entertainment in the form of their constant battle of personalities and eventual attraction to each other. *The Bone Collector* is a gripping story, portraying a man's will to live, a relationship between two people of totally different personalities, and, most importantly, the plot to find and neutralise a psychopath loose on the streets of New York.

> *e* This conclusion answers the question set, placing emphasis on how elements of the
> text appeal to the candidate. More marks could have been gained by addressing the
> issue of the appeal of stars generally, and of these stars in particular.

e The candidate shows a basic ability to present ideas within the conceptual framework but although there is a sound knowledge of the chosen text and some basic knowledge and understanding of media language, there is not enough detail about the appeal of the filmic qualities of *The Bone Collector* to an audience. Audience as a concept is not addressed well and institutional factors could have been developed further. There is too much descriptive story-telling at the expense of a detailed reading — the answer needs more focus on the language of the moving image and the codes and conventions embodied in the text. Overall, the answer would fall within the band for a grade **C**.

Film and broadcast fiction (II)

Discuss some of the ways in which formulas are repeated in film and/or television texts, and account for the popularity of this practice.

■ ■ ■

Grade-A answer

In his work about situation comedy, Grote, a media theorist, noted that 'things never change'. This is not just within individual programmes; the same formulas are used by sitcom producers everywhere. Copying previous formats gives producers something to draw ideas from and also to evaluate their own work against. It gives the audience a sense of familiarity with the slapstick comedy they enjoy.

> *e* The essay starts with a relevant quotation and shows evidence of using the conceptual framework by considering audience and institution.

In black American sitcoms such as *The Cosby Show* or *The Fresh Prince of Bel-Air*, the characters are very similar. The family unit is built around a successful father and mother with quick-witted youngsters to provide the conflict that leads to comedy. The young audience for *The Fresh Prince of Bel-Air* takes pleasure in the amicable conflict between the generations and the ways in which the younger characters are 'cool'. The family home and the workplace provide the realistic but rather mundane settings which enable the producers' and actors' comic intentions to come to the fore. A more outlandish and unusual setting might hold too much of the audience's attention.

> *e* This paragraph makes three good points by discussing the convention of stock characters, conflict and domestic location in situation comedy. The candidate evaluates confidently, referring to audience and institution.

British sitcoms tend to appeal to the dry wit of the audience — the jokes are a lot less 'in your face' but they are based on character humour too. Another repeated feature is the trend of British sitcoms to focus on failure. Basil Fawlty, Victor Meldrew and other characters' lives are a succession of painful and unsuccessful experiences. It seems that for a British audience watching someone else suffer makes their own lives seem much better.

> *e* Thorough knowledge of the topic is shown here. The paragraph covers similarities and differences within the situation comedy genre concisely and an interesting point is made which relates to institutions, audience and ideology. It could be improved with some textual examples, however.

In Britain there is evidence that younger people are beginning to tire of this old formula, and this opposition has led to a new formula that has been repeated several times already. It involves the low-key observation of 'ordinary' characters, who are not doing a great deal, such as in *The Royle Family* or more recently *The Office*. The way these are filmed is different from older sitcoms, with *The Office* using the conventions of a documentary, such as characters talking to the camera, even looking over their shoulders as they walk.

> *e* The candidate clearly understands that genres change and gives a good reference to media language, but misses an opportunity to expand the point on audience opposition.

In terms of the big screen, films often work with a narrative technique that has now become known as the classic narrative structure. Once again, this is a tried-and-tested formula for the producer. A simple structure of beginning, middle and end in chronological order makes script-writing much easier than an alternative narrative such as *Swordfish* (2001) (starring John Travolta), which starts at the end and is told in flashback. The classic narrative structure is used so commonly that a number of theories can be applied to it. Todorov identifies the beginning as a stage of equilibrium where everything is in order. This equilibrium is then disrupted, creating a problem or enigma, which elicits the interest of the audience, which is captivated as to how the equilibrium can be restored. Harmony is invariably reinstated at the end; the new equilibrium leaves everyone satisfied, which is ultimately what the audience wants from a cinematic experience.

> *e* The candidate demonstrates a critical understanding of theory and the popularity of conventional narrative patterns for producers and audiences, with an example of a film that does not conform to the formula and is therefore more problematic to produce.

Another theory, this time by Propp, identifies some interesting character roles which producers apply to many films. The classic narrative always features a hero, such as Tom Cruise in *Minority Report* (2002) or Bruce Willis in *Die Hard** (1988), with whom the audience's sympathies lie. He always defeats a villainous character and saves the princess (James Bond is another good example). This familiarity and satisfactory ending pleases the audience. However, the classic narrative is so well used that people know what will happen. The narrative becomes boring and does not stimulate and the film then has to rely on special effects to succeed. Without that the film falls apart.

> *e* An example would be useful here, but the candidate is building up the argument that formulas cannot be repeated endlessly and implying that producers are aware that younger and sophisticated audiences may become bored.

Not only are narrative formulas re-used but camera techniques are too, such as the classic Hollywood opening where the audience is shown an establishing shot of the city which then zooms in until it reaches the star of the film. Again, lack of variation can lead to such shots lacking impact and becoming rather clichéd, but increasingly producers are giving new twists to these ideas to improve this factor. The extreme speed of the take on this classic opening in *Run Lola Run** (1998) is an example of how a pattern is broken. So, while certain conventions are repeated, producers know that developments need to be made to maintain a fresh approach that will appeal to younger audiences.

e More relevant material is discussed here, focusing on camera work and how cinematic formulas have been altered to maintain audience interest. A sound conclusion is reached, which focuses on the question set.

e **This is a confident conceptual exploration and a well-developed discussion. The candidate demonstrates critical understanding of ideas and theories and covers television and film with good examples. The candidate shows clear understanding of narrative structure and generic conventions. This is a confident evaluation and personal response which would achieve a grade A.**

■ ■ ■

Grade-C answer

Films often use popular formulas. Many people have studied films and looked at the patterns they form. Propp looked at folk tales and analysed the characters within them and this can be applied to films. He believed that there were certain characters in every story — villain, hero, princess, donor etc. I studied *American Beauty** (1999) and *East is East* (1999).

e This is a satisfactory start — the candidate makes a clear point about narrative formula, indicating awareness of a relevant theory.

American Beauty does not conform to Propp's theory. Lester, the main character and narrator of the film, often scares the audience and from Jane's point of view he could be seen to be the villain (he is unfriendly and unconcerned towards her). However, Propp defines the hero as the main character on a quest and Lester fits into both these categories. If Lester is seen as the hero, then his wife could be seen as the villain as she makes his life miserable, for example yelling 'Lester, could you make me any later?'

e The candidate gives a useful illustration, in the form of a quotation from the text when applying Propp's character roles to a film.

Ricky could be the donor as he introduces Lester to the world of smoking and a more relaxed lifestyle (quitting his job). However, Angela could also be seen to be the donor as she makes Lester realise that there is beauty left in the world and gives him something to want and aspire to, convincing him to change.

e This paragraph illustrates the same point and does not develop the application of theory to the question. It would have been more relevant to discuss the development of formulas and to say something further about the film itself from the point of view of ideology and institution. The candidate should have applied the conceptual framework more rigorously, making reference to the relevance of narrative structure to audiences or producers.

East is East is a little more clearly defined. George is represented in a negative light. He upsets his children's lives by forcing them into arranged marriages and even making Sajid undergo circumcision late in life. This, however, is representing his religion, rather than himself, in a negative light, at least until the end when he beats his wife and children. Considering this, Ella and the children are the 'princesses' in need of rescuing from George's ways and fists. There are no clear other characters which fit into Propp's theories in this film, proving it to be of little use in both *American Beauty* and *East is East*.

> The candidate shows a sound understanding of Propp's theory, but starts with the theory rather than the text itself. We have no evidence that the text has been studied as a film as there is no reference to filmic language.

Todorov believed in a structured beginning, middle and end. At the start, there is equilibrium: the family is happy and everything is 'normal'. Disequilibrium sees the normality disrupted by something — this must be solved by realisation and action. Finally, a new equilibrium is established when everything returns to a new form of normality. In both the films this concept only works to an extent. The start of *American Beauty* shows Lester as he has lived for many years, his wife cutting roses, Lester 'jerking-off' in the shed etc. This is the state of equilibrium he lives in, although no one is truly happy. The state of disequilibrium begins as Lester starts to change his life by changing his job, smoking pot and working out, upsetting his wife. Equilibrium is never really established again as everything has changed and Lester is shot. This is where *American Beauty* has used the enigma code. The audience does not know what happens after he is shot, who gets the blame, or what happens to Jane and Ricky. The producers have done this deliberately in order to leave the viewers with questions in their minds, leaving a lasting impression. If the film continued it would become part of the crime genre and would not fit in with the aims of the film — to shock and entertain.

> The basic ideas of another narrative theorist, Todorov, are applied to the text, showing clear understanding of the story and a useful reference to the enigma code (which comes from Barthes). The candidate presents ideas within the conceptual framework by referring to the audience and producers. However, these ideas and the reference to the genre and aims of the films which connect with institution and ideology are not developed.

East is East also only uses Todorov's formula to an extent. The start shows the family happily integrated into a community. George is also happy at this point and the children running around the house in a frenzy shows the everyday life of the family. The disequilibrium could be said to be a gradual change — one son runs away, circumcision and arranged marriages are enforced, thus gradually upsetting the family. This film uses the enigma code too. It could be said that equilibrium is restored at the end, with Ella and George standing in the chip shop. Ella offers George a cup of tea, symbolising her love for him, and George replies with his usual 'half a cup', suggesting they will return to normal. This leaves the audience with questions about whether they will get back together, what happens to the children and whether George changes his ways. The ending is done purposely by the producers, leaving the members of the audience to reach their own conclusions. This encourages audience participation and discussion and makes people want to see it again to make their minds up.

> *e* The candidate applies the same theory to another film. No new points are made and the evaluation of the producers' reasons for an open ending is not developed to discuss the different ideologies of Ella and George and why a 'happy-ever-after' closure would be inappropriate. This paragraph offers a rather simplistic treatment of an interesting possibility.

A story's narrative often runs in chronological order, making it easy for audiences to understand it. This occurs in *East is East*, and helps to enforce its melodramatic mood and simple form. However, this is not true of some films, such as *Pulp Fiction* and *American Beauty*. *American Beauty* starts with a video clip which we see again much later in the film. This gives the audience a 'red herring', suggesting that they should believe that Lester's daughter killed him. The audience is surprised when this turns out not to be true, giving extra shock appeal. It also gives an insight into what will happen later, as Lester's voice-over tells the audience he is going to die in under a year. This makes the viewers continually look for clues as to why — it is always in the back of their minds. There is also the use of Lester's fantasies signified by roses and oriental music which gives a dreamy atmosphere. This does not run in line with the theory of linear action. Although *American Beauty* is almost an 'arthouse' film in style and doesn't follow a popular formula, the publicity and the stars generated large audiences that found it unusual and exciting.

> *e* This is a strong paragraph in which the candidate explains why the linear narrative pattern is broken in one particular film. However, the question indicates that some general conclusions need to be made.

East is East conforms more to the formulas and has a melodramatic, *Coronation Street* style. This is typical of a British production. The unusual side, the lack of closure at the end, is perhaps a result of it being a Film Four production as Film Four often supports alternative productions.

> *e* This short paragraph is underdeveloped, although it serves to show the candidate's awareness of the institution behind the film.

> *e* **This answer demonstrates sound knowledge of three narrative theories and applies them to two films. There is a basic use of appropriate terminology, such as voice-over, enigma and closure, but the discussion is not developed conceptually and the answer is restricted to narrative theories. The candidate does not evaluate the popularity of the practices. It could be that he/she has prepared an answer to a question from an earlier examination paper but hasn't adapted the material to this question. The knowledge and understanding of narrative and the application of theories to the chosen texts would put this response in the C band.**

Advice

Some questions, such as Question 1 above, ask for a reading of one or two film or broadcast texts. Others may ask for some sort of comparison between film and broadcast texts. Obviously you cannot, in the time available, provide much detail of the texts within your answer, but you should show that you have studied the language of the moving image through brief references to shots, scenes or filmic conventions.

The more recent the texts you write about, the more engaged your response is likely to be. Even though there are textbooks written about classic films, this exam tests your ability to apply the media studies perspective to the films you have studied. You must think about the audience and the institution concerned, the values and the ideologies embedded in the text, and the ways in which the language of the moving image conveys the meanings.

Question 3

Documentary

Why are reality TV-type documentary formats so popular with audiences and producers? Give examples of a range of programmes.

Grade-A answer

Reality TV has been a huge success in recent years. Touched upon by the BBC many years ago when the series *Video Diaries* gave the control of filming and editing to ordinary people, a lot has changed now. Today, popular reality TV shows like *Big Brother* and *I'm A Celebrity...Get Me Out of Here* involve set-up situations and the participants are carefully selected and far more controlled by producers.

> *e* The essay starts with an argument about producer control. There is a sense of a developing argument which will focus on the question 'why?' Three texts have been mentioned already, as have elements of the documentary topic: editing, set-ups, selection and control. It is important to use the topic terminology fluently like this.

Reality TV by its very nature deals with domestic issues, the ordinary real life of the viewers. Docu-soaps, for example, document an everyday place, or one the audience has been to before, and the everyday life of the staff is mixed with the everyday problems of the workplace, none of which are particularly outrageous. The word 'documentary' means factual, real or true, although no media product can ever be absolutely real.

> *e* This paragraph demonstrates good understanding of docu-soap and makes reference to the important topic debate about whether reality can ever be achieved.

However, producers also have, and use, the power to dramatise these issues, making a docu-soap more entertaining. The dramatic, character-led narratives in soap operas appeal to audiences and so producers keep this format in mind when making factual programmes. In *Airport*, for example, when a problem arises, technical devices are used to dramatise it. For example, in one programme a girl forgets her passport, but a friend gets it to her just in time. The use of a voice-over, controlling how the visuals are read by the audience, is important. Constant references to the lack of time, heard over shots of the girl sat thinking — perhaps only of her pet dog, but as the audience sees it, of her situation — together with fast cut shots and fast panning creates a sense of panic and suspense in the audience. There is, of course, the happy ending of the passport getting there on time, but because this is reality the audience is kept interested because there might not be a happy ending. It's not as predictable as fiction. This dramatisation of domestic issues is very similar to that of a soap opera.

e This is a detailed example which refers to media language and the documentary convention of voice-over. The candidate clearly understands the generic ingredients of the docu-soap and keeps the question in mind throughout.

The issue of a lost passport is not just entertaining. It is has a reality for the viewers, who can all identify with the situation; it could and may have happened to many of the audience members and is a thought that would have crossed their minds many times. They may even have been in the actual airport and this adds to their enjoyment. This fits in with the uses and gratifications theory of identification as an appeal. The producers shoot hours of film before they find a dramatic incident which will be suitable for the programme; they select from what has happened.

e The candidate focuses here on the argument about the role of the producer in mediating reality to make an interesting and entertaining programme for viewers. The reference to theory is helpful.

Reality TV programmes in the style of *999* can be very cheap to make, as using existing footage means that nothing needs to be shot. Many of these programmes are shown on Bravo, the same channel as pornography. The voyeurism of seeing something awful is usually masked by producers to stop their audiences feeling guilty about enjoying such programmes. As an example, *999* claims to have an educational slant to it, and *Crimewatch* goes as far as suggesting that watching the show helps to solve society's ills in the 'crime solving' element of the programme.

e The candidate offers a strong personal response in this paragraph and makes a good point about the appeal of voyeurism, audience pleasure in observing disasters and how it can be disguised as educational. Reference to two different documentaries illustrates the point.

Such programmes also keep the same optimism as *Airport*, despite the nature of what they show. *Crimewatch* does this by stressing the cases which the programme and its viewers have solved, while *999* uses examples where the narrative has a happy ending — the victim survives. This optimism appeals to the audience, but also adds the ideology of community and individual heroism to that of living in the very dangerous society suggested by the programmes' content. This community ideology is dominant and is seen in soap operas too. Marxist theory suggests that institutions portray this ideology to maintain the status quo of the mass audience, ensuring the dominance of the rich and powerful. Perhaps institutions influence the producers to do this through reality TV.

e The candidate presents a very strong argument in this paragraph. It could be contested, but the candidate supports the point about ideology by referring to other television formats and backing it up with theory.

Big Brother was a phenomenon, being one of the first programmes to involve audience interaction. The interaction of voting by phone had a real appeal to audiences, and the call cost and text message costs made the producers a fair amount of money on top of what the programme was already making. The selection of contestants meant aspirational ones could be chosen. Kate and Spencer are just two examples of beautiful people in the third series.

> *Another text is given, with a useful reference to appeal to audience and producers of audience interaction by voting. The point about selection is backed up with an example.*

Like a soap opera, docu-soaps can follow the same segmented narrative, going from one situation to another, as happens in *Big Brother* where voice-overs make mini-narratives which form a larger one. This appeals to inattentive television audiences who can pick up on the programme at any time. Reality TV fulfils many of the uses and gratifications specifications, even education, as it deals with real domestic issues. These shows are cheap to make with no stars to pay, yet audiences relate to some characters as stars, for example making Jeremy from *Airport* a celebrity. Reality TV, therefore, has a huge appeal to both audiences and producers.

> *This paragraph sums up the argument. It includes further evidence of understanding of topic terminology and makes an additional point about the inexpensiveness of new reality TV formats.*

> **This essay is a confident conceptual exploration and shows a detailed knowledge of hybrid forms of documentary. Notice how all the Key Concepts are covered and integrated within the discussion of the question. Note too that the candidate has covered a range of different reality TV formats, demonstrating breadth of study. The argument is supported by textual detail and theoretical references. Overall, this essay would be marked at the top of the band for grade A.**

Grade-C answer

Big Brother has achieved phenomenal success with its depiction of what people are really like when placed into a new environment with strangers. Reality TV is big business in an age where people are becoming more and more interested in simply watching how people cope in different situations. Programmes like *Big Brother* give viewers the chance to participate in the voting process; this helps them feel more involved in the programme. Being able to view any room in the house, see people when they are at their most vulnerable and see them when they are in the diary room confessing their inner feelings gives us a feeling of superiority and power. Programmes such as *Survivor, I'm A Celebrity...Get Me Out of Here* and even the whole *Pop Idol/Popstars* phenomenon all have that element of audience participation and voyeurism.

> *The candidate wastes no time in getting to the point of the question and suggests audience participation and voyeurism as the reasons for the popularity of reality TV with audiences. Appropriate terminology is used. A good point is made about*

the feelings of power and superiority audiences have when watching *Big Brother* which demonstrates understanding of relevant ideas and theories.

Reality TV is popular simply because it is advertised to us as being 'real' and this is enough to get the attention of many people as everyone is able to gain some amount of pleasure from being able to watch a total stranger and criticise their flaws and faults. In a way it almost brings people together. When the last series of *Big Brother* was shown there was rarely anywhere you could go to escape the question: 'Did you see *Big Brother* last night?' But, in much the same way, it separates its audience into groups who support different people in the show.

e This is a simple personal response. It could be developed by exploring what 'real' means and why this ideal of reality appeals to audiences, and by exploring the concept of audience in more detail. The use of the second person 'you' is too personal. The candidate would do better to discuss who the audience for these shows is and which institution(s) broadcast them and why.

Docu-soaps also became very popular in 2002 when nearly every single channel had a docu-soap at any one point. For example, BBC1 had *Paddington Green* and *Airport*; ITV had *Shampoo* and *Airline*; Channel 4 had *Big Brother* and *Model Behaviour*. Each of these had characters who seemed to be almost too exaggerated to be real. *Airport's* Jeremy Spake became so popular that he has now become a regular part of daytime television.

e Docu-soaps, a different type of reality TV, are listed. The candidate demonstrates that this format was popular with producers from different broadcasting institutions but no reason is given for this. This paragraph misses an opportunity for focusing on the question and applying the conceptual framework. It could also have discussed the appeal of character-driven documentaries and explained the 'soap-like' qualities.

The major problem with reality TV is that it simply isn't what it promises to be. In programmes such as *Survivor* and *Big Brother*, people acted up to the cameras — it was almost like watching an amateur dramatics performance. It also appears to leave you, the audience, to decide what you think of people in the show but then uses editing and camera positioning to make certain 'characters' more or less likeable through either selected footage or, in the case of programmes like *Paddington Green*, interviews where people come across as almost comic in their views and opinions.

e The candidate demonstrates some understanding of the issue of mediation, i.e. how the presence of cameras affects 'reality' — an important idea within the documentary topic. However, this material could have been made more relevant to the question and better integrated into the discussion.

The appeal of such programmes is clear in a sense, as it could be said that they offer companionship to those who watch (*Big Brother* includes 24-hour surveillance), and in shows such as *Popstars* we are able to see the selection process of the new big name in pop. There is a look to a show like *Big Brother* that adds to its appeal. Everything is seen as if through the eyes of a surveillance system, adding to the sense that it is real and that the contestants really don't know they are being watched — this adds to our sense of voyeurism.

I believe that reality TV has had such great success because it plays on the human enjoyment of voyeurism but also because of its use of audience participation.

e The candidate brings in some new ideas about the appeal of reality TV programmes to audiences, but the paragraphs would have been strengthened by some textual illustration.

e **This is a sound personal response in which the candidate demonstrates knowledge of a range of reality TV programmes and a consideration of debates relevant to the topic. He/she emphasises the appeal of such formats to audiences but the appeal for producers is not dealt with equally well. The answer would have been improved with more textual detail and discussion of documentary filming techniques used — as it is, it would fall within the band for grade C.**

Advice

Some questions may ask you to discuss a statement about documentaries, perhaps concerning issues of realism or manipulation. Whatever your opinion about a statement or quotation, remember that you must support your ideas with textual detail and references to documentaries you have studied. Watch a variety of documentaries, not just those studied in class, and make sure that you think about them in terms of their structure, the techniques used and the intentions of the documentary maker along with the conceptual framework.

Advertising and marketing

Why are covert advertising strategies used to promote products and brands? Illustrate your answer with examples of promotional techniques.

■ ■ ■

Grade-A answer

Covert strategies are becoming more widespread for many different reasons. As the cost of television airtime increases, companies can no longer afford to run new advertising campaigns every year. (This can be seen by the repetitive use of certain campaigns for several consecutive years.) As people have grown up in the media revolution they are more aware of advertising techniques and may not be as easily manipulated as they were 10 years ago. To combat this, advertising firms have had to come up with new ways to promote brands.

   e This introduction focuses on the question and gives two reasons for covert techniques. It is a confident start which shows understanding of the topic.

Product placement is one of the most recent covert advertising techniques and is highly visible in the new James Bond film. Within the film there is evidence of product placement for Aston Martin, Vodaphone and a watch company. This benefits the film-makers as they receive free props and costumes. In return, the companies receive effectively free advertising in cinemas across the world and in people's homes when the film comes out on VHS and DVD. It also has the effect of endorsement, leading people (particularly aspirers) into false needs and into believing that James Bond himself is personally endorsing the product.

   e The candidate evaluates product placement well and gives a reasonable example. The final sentence refers to needs and aspirers and shows critical understanding of theories and ideas related to advertising. The candidate demonstrates competent use of appropriate topic terminology, too.

This can be linked to celebrity endorsement which is becoming more widespread, particularly among sports stars who may have contracts allowing them to wear only certain brands of sportswear, e.g. Adidas has David Beckham, Reebok has Ryan Giggs. This gives the companies plenty of airtime when celebrities are wearing their products. Many people idolise sports stars and will wear what their heroes wear in a bid to be like them. As such stars are popular with the majority of society it helps to sell brands to mainstreamers (the majority of the population, according to cross-cultural consumer characteristics), and aspirers who want to become mainstreamers, and spend money on brands to become like them. The use of celebrities can also aid more traditional advertising techniques such as sex appeal and intertextuality as people may link products with programmes if the celebrity appears in both — for instance, Jamie Oliver appears in Sainsbury's adverts and in *Jamie's Kitchen*.

e The candidate brings forward another covert technique as part of the argument. Again, advertising ideas and terms like 'aspirers' and 'mainstreamers' are used with confidence and are related to the examples. By referring to traditional advertising techniques which are apparent in paid-for direct advertising, the candidate shows a convincing grasp of the topic and evidence of thorough study.

Sponsorship is big business, especially in football and Formula One, as both sports would go bankrupt without the sponsorship they receive from different companies. Watching a football match or a Grand Prix is effectively like sitting through a 2-hour advert as viewers are bombarded by brand names which are aimed at the assumed audience. This can be seen in the adverts run during the breaks, too. The products are aimed at men, e.g. cars, engine oil and razors. By sponsoring an event, like Coca-Cola sponsoring the World Cup, advertisers can use the sport as part of their brand image and include false values such as Coca-Cola being healthy, fun and as important as football (if football can be considered important). People do not automatically recognise these strategies as adverts, as companies are sponsoring the event or television programme. For example, Cadbury sponsors *Coronation Street* and the promise, pleasure and excitement of the soap opera is associated with the brand itself. This gives extra value to the brand.

e The candidate gives excellent examples of sponsorship and its advantages for the marketers. Again, audience reaction is explored.

Companies also support charities or schools to promote a warm, friendly face so people don't believe they are purely interested in making money. However, they don't do this because it makes them feel good, they do it as a public relations exercise to make the public like them and maybe encourage people to buy their products, which in turn provides them with relatively cheap advertising.

e This paragraph evaluates the advantages of another covert technique. This could be improved with an example, such as Tesco's computers for schools scheme.

Because advertising is becoming increasingly expensive, cutting costs is a priority so covert techniques are being used. The techniques used become stealthier as people become more aware of the manipulative power of the media.

e The conclusion is brief but expressed well, and focuses on the question.

e **This essay shows thorough knowledge and understanding of the functions and purposes of promotional strategies and techniques. Relevant concepts are applied and the use of examples is excellent. There are more promotional techniques which the candidate has not touched on, but the detail of the examples, the confident and well-developed argument and the critical understanding of theories relating to advertising and marketing techniques and audience theory would make this a good grade-A answer. There is clear critical autonomy here and the candidate avoids a 'list-like' approach by selecting material carefully.**

Grade-C answer

In today's age one particular brand faces competition from numerous other brands that are all targeting the same audience. We are now bombarded with literally thousands of adverts per day and on average we only spend 1.5 seconds looking at each one. Marketeers today have to ensure that their campaigns are unique so they will attract and persuade people.

> *e* The candidate starts with a definite statement which shows understanding of the advertising industry, although covert techniques are not mentioned.

The Nike campaign was called 'Just Do it'. This is called 'in-your-face' advertising. Although this could be portrayed as being arrogant, it expresses the attitude Nike has had over the years. For this campaign it used product endorsement by employing the major basketball star Michael Jordan to model its product. Product endorsement is a persuasive technique which many brands use. It entices the audience to buy the product because they believe that if the product is good enough for the professionals then it will certainly be good enough for them. Young people are particularly influenced by seeing their sporting heroes wearing or using certain products.

> *e* This is an old campaign and the candidate obviously does not have first-hand knowledge of the texts. It would have been better to use an example from a current Nike campaign. A point is made about the advantages of using celebrities to create audience identification, but it is not fully developed.

Sega was a brand that was specifically marketed to a young audience. Its manufacturers did not want to sell just the product. They wanted to sell the idea, lifestyle and attitude too. With the help of Sonic the Hedgehog, Sega soon became a fashion item and gave children a street credibility and a sense of belonging. They had bought into an attitude, an attitude which was fun. Merchandising was responsible for the huge interest and T-shirts, caps and even key rings.

> *e* Again, this is a dated example. A more recent example of merchandising would have been better, such as tie-ins between the Harry Potter films and clothing, stationery, chocolate etc. However, the candidate does show understanding of some topic ideas here by linking audience with the product.

Publicity is also useful because it gives opportunities for the stars in the campaign to make personal appearances and interviews so they can make people aware of the product. This happens in the film industry where the star of a film may appear in magazine articles and on television and radio chat shows. This is cheaper than paying for trailers and advertisements. 'Plugs' are useful for promoting people. An example of this is when Mis-teeq made an appearance on Channel 4's *So Graham Norton* a few days after the release of their second album. As a technique it works quite well as it isn't obvious advertising. Product placement is also highly effective. This involves the product being advertised in the *mise-en-scène*. For example, the new Nokia mobile phone was advertised in the film *The Matrix* (1999).

> ℓ Two covert techniques are mentioned. Publicity and plugs are evaluated with a good, contemporary example; product-placement has a useful example too. The candidate misses the intertextuality between the examples and could have added something here on audience and institution.

Careful market research must be carried out at first to ensure that there is a gap in the market and that there will be interest from the public.

> ℓ This is an accurate statement, but the answer is straying from the wording of the question.

Sponsorship is a way of promoting a brand. Cadbury sponsors *Coronation Street* and Jacob's Crackers *Who Wants to be a Millionaire?* Again, this keeps people aware of the product. There are also other forms of sponsorship, like football shirts; for example, Arsenal is sponsored by O_2 mobile phones.

> ℓ This very promising point is not developed. It should have formed a more prominent part of the answer as it is highly relevant to the discussion on why covert techniques are used. It would appear that the candidate has run out of time.

> ℓ **The candidate demonstrates knowledge of a range of strategies. There is some useful illustration, but some examples are rather old. The answer is not well structured and with better planning the candidate could have gained more marks. This essay would just come into the C band.**

Advice

Some questions may ask for more textual detail. However, merely giving a textual analysis of one or two advertisements is not enough; you still need to be able to contextualise the texts within their campaigns and be able to explain why the techniques are used. If a question asks you to write about an advertising or marketing campaign you have studied, remember to integrate the conceptual framework and your knowledge of marketing principles and practice in your answer. Don't just describe the campaign. Sometimes there are television programmes about advertising and marketing campaigns, but these are not structured from a media studies perspective; you will need to add this yourself.

British newspapers

How do tabloids address their readers? Give a range of examples to support your answer and outline the major differences between tabloids and broadsheet newspapers.

■ ■ ■

Grade-A answer

Tabloids are smaller than broadsheets and can be divided into two types. The graphology used in tabloid newspapers is similar to that used in gossip magazines. Links between the two include the emphasis on the use of pictures and large, bold typeface designed to attract attention and tell a story simply. Some tabloids are also known as 'red-top' newspapers. These are newspapers that are generally aimed at lower social classes (C2 to E) and have high levels of circulation in the UK. Examples of tabloids include the *Sun*, the *Mirror* and the *Star* and these three tabloids have many readers.

> *e* The candidate gives a clear definition of tabloids and an overview of the style of presentation. The reference to circulation and readership shows topic knowledge.

An example of a tabloid's news values can be illustrated by comparing the space a particular story takes up in a broadsheet and in a tabloid. On the day an IRA undercover agent had his cover blown, leaving him open to assassination, the *Telegraph* devoted half of its front page to the story with a large headline while the *Sun* had a small, half-page article on page 11.

> *e* The candidate's reference to news values shows competent use of appropriate terminology and is illustrated well with a recent example.

Tabloids like the *Sun* align themselves more with gossip magazines than serious news reportage. They have been accused of sensationalising stories and providing biased reports. For example, a story involving the boxer Audley Harrison was headlined 'BBC to blame...', showing an obvious opinion. The nature of newspaper reporting as a whole necessitates some form of opinion, but the *Sun* in particular leaves no scope for other interpretations by its readers who are expected to agree with what 'the *Sun* says', the title of its editorial. Many tabloids, including middle-market ones like the *Daily Mail*, start campaigns to get their readers involved, often by voting on issues like asylum seekers or the euro. Readers feel included and pleased to be able to express their views. Tabloid newspapers portray strong political views. For example, from 1994 the political propaganda of Rupert Murdoch's media (the owner of the *Sun* and *The Times*) enabled Tony Blair and the Labour Party's rise to power.

> *e* The candidate gives a thorough evaluation of the style, content and attitude of tabloids. There is a confident conceptual exploration, particularly of audience and institution, and a useful illustration of the treatment of a story.

The informal register and colloquial mannerisms used by tabloid journalists appeal to their target audience. Grammatical features found in tabloid newspaper articles include the use of slang, puns, alliteration and assonance, and stories are often light-hearted and humorous in tone. In addition, the simple sentences used are designed to be understood by the target readers, whose educational background is often fairly low. Tabloid subject matter is concerned more with gossip than with hard news. Readers use their newspaper for entertainment and the tabloids contain lots of stories about entertainment, with special editors and journalists who report on the show business industry. The content covers other media forms, such as television, film and popular music, and often reproduces interviews or gossip about celebrities. The tabloids can make or break celebrities to an extent. For example, criticising and then praising David Beckham, covering Naomi Campbell's drug problems and printing sneaky photographs of famous people not looking their best can have an effect on people's public images and careers.

e Here the candidate demonstrates detailed knowledge of tabloid style and content, with appropriate terminology. It would have been useful to include an example of a pun, alliteration, slang or assonance, but the contemporary references to celebrities are used well.

Such conventions are used because each newspaper needs to advertise itself to compete with the large variety of tabloids available in newsagents. This is the same for broadsheets too, and all newspapers lead on an exclusive if they have one. All newspapers offer sections aimed at different readers, like travel or business, and all newspapers have sports and entertainment pages. The content which tabloids emphasise is that of media forms (e.g. television, film, internet), celebrities, real-life stories and stories of national proximity. Tabloids seek stories about media and celebrities, and present these as exclusive, sensational and entertaining — news values that are likely to interest the target audience.

e The candidate keeps to the question by commenting on the similarities between tabloids and broadsheets. This paragraph considers the competitive nature of the institutions and shows understanding of the contemporary news industry.

In contrast, broadsheets place their emphasis on the informative content of their stories. They are generally aimed at the higher social classes (A to C1), which means that their readership is smaller than that of the tabloids. Broadsheets often incorporate a number of sections including business, politics, arts including theatre and classical music, international news and travel. They tend to use more complex sentences than their tabloid rivals with the emphasis on fact rather than on opinion. The news values of both types of newspapers are concerned with dramatic stories, negativity, proximity and real-life issues, with the broadsheets concentrating on current affairs and worldwide news. The differences in news values of these two types of paper can be seen in their content. Tabloids concentrate on celebrities, e.g. 'Les Dennis close to suicide'; sex, e.g. Jordan's new boyfriend; and sport, e.g. Beckham's broken foot in the World Cup. Broadsheets, on the other hand, concentrate on world-wide news, e.g. war on terror; and business, e.g. house prices continue to rise.

> *e* This paragraph concludes the essay by referring to the contrast between the content, style and news values of broadsheets and tabloids.

> *e* **The candidate shows thorough knowledge and understanding of tabloid and broadsheet newspapers and covers the areas of content, layout and style. There is a good emphasis on readers and the Key Concepts are kept in mind throughout the essay. References to news values are well integrated and the answer shows the ability to give a wide range of examples of newspaper content and stories. There is thorough understanding of some relevant ideas and debates about the topic area. The candidate develops some points in detail, showing a good personal response. Overall, the essay would achieve a solid grade A.**

■ ■ ■

Grade-C answer

Tabloids are the newspapers which are seen as being for the lower socioeconomic groups. They tend to deal more with gossip than news. Examples of tabloids are the *Mirror*, the *Star*, the *Sun* and the *Daily Sport*. Broadsheet papers like the *Telegraph* are likely to deal more with hard news as their readers, from the higher socioeconomic groups, are more interested in money matters and international news. This is true except if there is a war, such as in Iraq, when all newspapers will cover it.

> *e* This is a good start which clearly differentiates the news and entertainment value difference between tabloids and broadsheets. The candidate outlines different readerships briefly. The last sentence refers to a current example and shows a sound personal response which could have been developed further.

Tabloids present the news to their readers using informal language and unsophisticated words. They also use slang and nicknames in their stories. Broadsheets use formal language and sophisticated words even though some of the stories are the same as in tabloids.

> *e* The candidate makes a point about informal language, but without illustration it cannot show personal study of actual newspapers. The comment about some stories being the same is good, but the opportunity to account for this in terms of news values is missed. For a question such as this, textual illustrations may be brief, but to gain high marks each point should have an example to show case-study knowledge.

The headlines found in tabloid newspapers are very simple and each word is usually only one syllable long. For example, when Michael Jackson dangled his baby over a balcony the *Sun* used the headline 'Mad Bad Dad'. The headlines used in broadsheets, however, are usually a sentence long and they brief the reader about what the story is concerning (e.g. 'Ricin found in south London flat').

> *e* This is a good example of the differences between tabloids and broadsheets. However, the comparison is not discussed fully and far more could have been said about the Michael Jackson story — how certain celebrities make news copy for tabloids, for example.

Tabloids also differ from broadsheets because they are more concerned with the individuals involved in a story whereas broadsheets look at the issue surrounding it. For example, the tabloid newspapers reported the recent developments in Operation Ore by concentrating on Pete Townshend and his life rather than on the issues surrounding the operation.

> *e* Another difference is outlined with a recent example. The news value relating to personalisation is implied but not explored. There is sound understanding here, but the readers are not referred to.

Tabloids are also concerned with sensationalism whereas broadsheet newspapers are concerned with facts and information. Several stories reported by tabloid newspapers have later turned out to be false. This is because the newspapers were more concerned with making a sensational exclusive than ensuring that the facts were correct. An example of this was when the *News of the World* printed information about a so-called 'known paedophile'. The information turned out to be incorrect and an innocent man was accused.

> *e* Again, sound knowledge is demonstrated, but the focus should have been on how the tabloids address their readers.

Tabloids tend to include little foreign news and most contain gossip. Broadsheet papers seem to concentrate more on foreign news. Although there are many differences between the two types of newspaper, rules about what news is presented is the same for both. Both types have to abide by certain legal restrictions and the code of conduct set by the Press Complaints Commission. This can affect what news is reported and what is not. Another factor affecting which stories go into a paper and which stay out is the 'gatekeeper'. This is usually the owner or the editor of the paper and his or her personal views on an issue can affect how a story is reported. A common example of this is at election time when the papers put across their views on each party. Ostracising can also affect what stories are reported. If a certain establishment (e.g. a football club) is reported badly in a newspaper, the club may not share other news with that particular paper. This gives other newspapers an advantage and as the institutions that produce these papers are in a readership battle, they want all the exclusives they can get.

> *e* Time seems to be running out, and the candidate falls into the trap of remembering everything that has been learned about the topic. Much of this is rather confused and doesn't relate to the question asked. Planning an essay before starting would avoid this last-minute inclusion of irrelevant material.

In conclusion, although the stories presented to the reader by the tabloid and broadsheet newspapers are similar, the way in which they are presented and the way the reader is addressed is very different.

e The concluding sentence sums up the argument.

e **The essay shows adequate understanding of tabloid techniques. The candidate gives some effective textual examples, though not all points are illustrated in equal detail. There is a clear understanding of the differences between tabloid and broadsheet newspapers but the issue of how the reader is addressed is rather neglected. There are references to relevant topic information, including news values, and a sound personal response is evident in the use of examples. The answer would be in band C. With more illustration and focus, the answer would go into a higher mark band.**

Advice

Always use current examples. National newspapers are printed every day and online versions are updated several times a day. Don't rely on textbooks — instead, apply what you have learnt in class and in textbooks to contemporary news stories. If you are studying British newspapers as a topic, you should read them regularly. Buy a range of newspapers when there is an important story and compare how they cover it. For example, you could look at the differences in how a national broadsheet, a national tabloid and a local evening paper address one or more of the following: war, a major crime, an issue relating to the government or a politician, a celebrity scandal or a natural disaster. When writing about stories you have read yourself, you will be able to show a clear and engaged personal response.

Remember to analyse stories using the conceptual framework. Think about the readers, the owners, the values and ideology of the stories and the newspaper generally, the genre of the paper and the codes and conventions relevant to the genre, how individuals, social groups or nations are represented in the newspapers (sports coverage is useful here) and, of course, have detailed knowledge of the meanings conveyed by the language of the print medium, including analysis of pictures and their captions. Some questions may ask your opinion of a statement made about the British press, for example whether newspapers distort the news, or whether the freedom to print what they like should be curtailed. You must always support your argument with textual illustrations and it should clearly come from a media studies perspective. Unsubstantiated personal rants do not earn many marks.

Practice questions

In the exam there will be two questions under each topic and you will be required to answer one question from each of the two topics you have studied. Below are some additional essay titles for you to practise. The best way to use these questions is as follows:

- Use each one to help you prepare for the exam. Work out how you can best show your knowledge of the topic, your understanding of the Key Concepts and the detailed case studies you have made during your course.
- Practise writing timed essays, aiming to be able to show all you know in an appropriate way in just 45 minutes per question. You may need to take more time at first, allowing yourself time to plan carefully and even check up on some facts, terminology or theories before you start. However, once you have used this method, do the other topic essays in the correct amount of time.
- When you are ready to do a proper timed essay, allow yourself 5 minutes for planning and then check the question wording again before starting to write. When you have finished writing, wait until the next day before reading it. They try to assess its strengths and weaknesses.
- When you check your work, treat it like one of the sample essays in this guide and study it in detail. Highlight the good parts, as you may be able to use them again, and rewrite the weaker sections, including any textual detail, terminology or focus on the question that would improve your answer.

Film and broadcast fiction

(1) Discuss *one* film or *one* broadcast fictional text that you think offers more than entertainment to its audience. Give detailed illustrations in your answer.

(2) Compare *two different types* of broadcast narrative and explain how each type appeals to its target audience. Provide textual illustration in your answer.

(3) 'All films tell stories.' Refer in detail to *two* films of your choice to discuss some of the main storytelling techniques used by film makers.

Documentary

(1) Compare two *different types* of documentary and give reasons for the differences between them. Include textual illustration in your answer.

(2) Can documentaries ever represent reality? Illustrate with reference to a *range of documentary material*.

(3) John Grierson stressed that 'dramatisation' was an element that distinguished documentary from other forms of non-fiction film. Describe and account for the use of 'dramatisation' in *two* documentaries of your choice. At least *one* of the documentaries must have been made *before 1990*.

Advertising and marketing

(1) How do advertisers and marketers get their campaigns for a brand or product talked about? Discuss the strategies used in a campaign of your choice and evaluate their success.

(2) 'Adverts don't sell products — they sell brands.' How far do you agree with this statement? In your answer give detailed illustrations from a campaign or campaigns of your choice.

(3) Describe and evaluate the appeal to target audiences of a range of *three* advertising and/or marketing techniques. Provide examples in your answer.

British newspapers

(1) Does the British press attempt to influence readers' opinions? Refer to examples of news stories and features in your argument.

(2) Compare *two* British newspapers, one a local newspaper, and account for the differences in the selection, construction and presentation of news.

(3) Why do people still read newspapers? Present a detailed reading of *one* newspaper and discuss how it appeals to its readers.